SECONDARY SCHOOL

ASSEMBLIES

- FOR BUSY TEACHERS -

VOL 1

CheckPoint
Press

SECONDARY SCHOOL ASSEMBLIES FOR BUSY TEACHERS Vol I

ISBN-13: 978-0-906628-35-2

Published by CheckPoint Press, Ireland

CheckPoint Press
Books With Something to Say..

email: editor@checkpointpress.com

Website: www.checkpointpress.com

Cover and illustrations by Julie Hayes

SECONDARY SCHOOL ASSEMBLIES

FOR BUSY TEACHERS

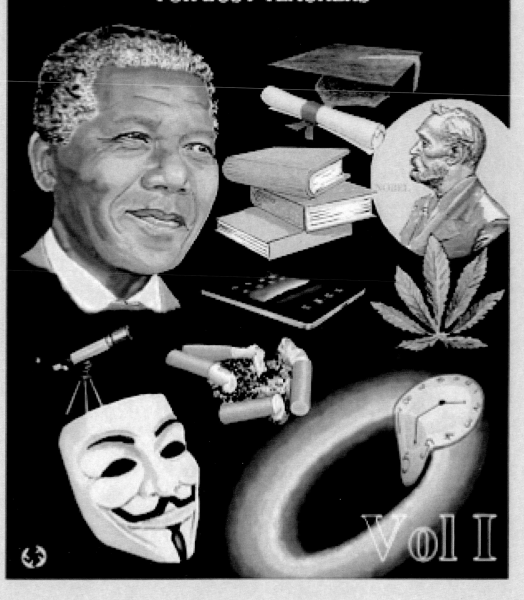

Vol I

INTRODUCTION

All of the assemblies in here are ready to go!

We know that those lucky enough to be presenting an assembly on a Monday morning haven't always had the time to plan and prepare a masterpiece. This is where this book comes in.

We would, of course, recommend reading the material through first, because a little practice does wonders for any delivery.

Do read the sections underlined before beginning as these are instructions, guidelines or suggestions for the presenter.

But if the worst comes to the worst, and you have only had time to briefly survey the contents, you can grab this little book, go into your assembly hall and simply read one out.

However, if you are in this much of a rush, it may be better to skip the 'audience interaction' bits, because once your students join in you really need to know where you are going!

While being predominantly secular, all of these assemblies have a celebratory and enquiring attitude to life, reinforcing positive values and attitudes to one's self and others.

Enjoy!

Contents.

How to Structure an Assembly.. 6

Assemblies:

HOW TO STRUCTURE AN ASSEMBLY

Speaking in public is not like other forms of communication. Speakers are often unaware, or just don't give enough thought to the ways in which public speaking differs from other forms of communication. Most untrained presenters soon realize that public speaking can be a very nerve-wracking experience, and that there is a real risk of making a fool of themselves.

Being aware of what makes public speaking different from the other ways in which we communicate with each other will help you understand what you need to do in order to give a great assembly.

Speaking to large groups of people on formal occasions presents a set of unique problems; so this situation must be dealt with differently.

1. How an Assembly differs from a conversation:

a) It is harder to command your audience's attention than when talking with two or three people because, unlike in a chat, the people who are listening to you <u>do not expect to have to contribute</u>; *they may switch off!*

b) In a small, informal group, you are rarely expected to be the expert, or to necessarily to come out with some pearl of wisdom. But in a speaking engagement (which is what an assembly really is) you are supposed to be worth listening to – that's why you have been given the privilege of the stage.

2. How an Assembly is not the same as simply handing out a document:

It is harder to command your audience's attention than if you had given them something to read because, unlike reading a document or a book, the people listening to you <u>cannot go back</u> and check something they didn't hear properly or understand. So if they don't 'get it' loud and clear the first time, you will lose them.

So you really are up against it a bit. The assembled students can just sit there in judgement of you; they can ignore you; they can secretly laugh at you; or they can fail to pay you any attention whatsoever.

And you may not even know it!

So mostly, this book is about interesting content. We have written what we believe is some compelling, topical material.

But we must always remember that form and content are interlinked.

Here are a few pointers for a great presentation.

<u>Movement</u>

Avoid being completely predictable in your movement: don't stay in the same place the whole time, especially if this involves being stuck behind a table or a lectern.

Make clear decisive movements: a clear decisive movement in almost any direction will make your audience sit up and take notice. Try to do it at significant points in your delivery. It will look as though you are moved (literally) by your own words. However, don't keep repeating the same movement such as pacing backwards and forwards, as this quickly becomes obvious and/or distracting.

Look at Them!

Make eye contact as much as possible and scan the whole room. Don't just look at the front or the back, the right or the left, or at just one or two friendly faces. Systematically scan the room, and give the audience the feeling you are talking to each of them personally.

Passion

Always, always, always speak as if you are deeply serious about your message. Make it seem that it means a lot to you. If it doesn't mean much to *you*, then why should *they* listen? Never for example say something casual like; *" I knew I had to do assembly today so I looked on the internet for something to talk about."* It undermines you, and undermines the material you are presenting.

Stories

A great way to deal with an assembly is to have a story at its heart. People love listening to anecdotes, especially well-constructed ones, and it gives you a central theme to hang everything else around.

Structure

Follow a clearly defined route.

We have structured the assemblies in this book as follows:

- Opening Hook
- Overview
- One/Two/Three Main Points
- Summary
- Closing

1. Opening – start with a 'hook' - something to make them sit up and take notice.

   As a public speaker, you should always be looking for ways to make your audience listen; to catch and hold their attention. Telling them that something is unique about any particular assembly is a great way to start. Other classic openings are the use of a rhetorical question; an amazing fact; an interesting story or a famous quotation.

2. Introduction and Overview – Tell them generally what you are going to tell them, without giving it all away.

3. The Body of the Assembly – One, Two or Three Main Points with clear links between them. Links are very important. They are like signposts for your audience which bind the presentation together and give it cohesion and meaning.

4. Summary – Tell them again briefly, what you've already told them. Hit all the main points again.

5. Closing – A mirror of the Opening; something with a bit of drama, humour or punch! Don't forget to thank the students for their time and attention.

1

ENERGY

 *AIM: To encourage Green thinking and actions, this assembly explains in a clear and succinct way, the reality of Global Warming and gives practical tips on how students can help the situation at their own level.*

OPENING HOOK

Think of the thing you would most like to be doing at this very moment. I can guarantee that whatever it is you are thinking of, it will require energy of some sort. Energy is needed for *everything*.

OVERVIEW

Today, I want us to think for just a few moments about the problems the world faces with all the energy we have to use. It's an unimaginable amount. We're going to think about these issues and we're going to look at what you and your family can do start helping with this problem right now.

MAIN POINT ONE – WE'RE RUNNING OUT OF ENERGY

The problem we have is that the world is running out of easily-useable energy. Most of the energy we use involves burning dead things: oil gas and coal are all products derived from dead creatures.

The total amount of oil used since the 1800's is approximately 250 billion barrels. Total known oil reserves are approximately 250 billion barrels. So sooner or later we are going to run out of oil. The same applies to gas, coal and nuclear fuel. These are all non-renewable sources of energy - they cannot be replaced.

Today's society relies on energy. Without cheap, easily available energy, we would not have modern transport, industry or food. In fact most of the population of the world would starve.

I want you to think about what it would be like trying to live without electricity or gas in your home.

The gases produced by burning fossil fuels are causing global warming. This is not a theory; this is as close to a fact as science can get. It is agreed by nearly every independent scientist in the world.

It is now possible to measure the amount of carbon dioxide that used to be in our atmosphere in the past. We can go back hundreds of thousands of years by taking core samples of the ice in Antarctica. Because as each layer of snow was compacted to ice, bubbles of air from that particular time were trapped inside the ice.

Scientists have drilled down into the ground and taken samples of the ice from each layer finding out how much carbon dioxide was in the air at that time. They have then compared the amount of carbon dioxide in the air with the fossil records for that time.

In every case, whenever the carbon dioxide levels rose there were mass extinctions on the earth - in some cases nearly all life was made extinct.

The level of carbon dioxide now is *fifty times higher* than it has ever been in the past. If we do not stop producing carbon dioxide it is likely that all life on earth will become extinct.

The world is addicted to energy but there are other ways of producing energy rather than burning dead things.

I would like you to think about the following:

(Taken from the orders of magnitude website)

Every second, the sun produces more energy than human civilizations have ever used in history.

The sun is the ultimate Nuke. It produces the same amount of energy in 1 second as 1 trillion megaton atom bombs.

Enough energy falls on the Sahara desert as light to supply all of Western Europe's energy needs.

The yearly electricity consumption of the world is 5.67×10^{19} J. That is a lot! 5.6 with eighteen zeroes on the end.

The total energy from the sun that strikes the world each second is 1.5×10^{22} J. And that's an awful lot!

So we have far more energy reaching the world every day from the sun than the total electricity consumed by the world in a year.

I have to ask a question. With all of this free energy around why are we still burning dead things to power our cars, homes and everything else?

The answer is possibly that it has been easy and cheap to dig up and burn dead things. There are also lots of vested interests, particularly in the energy companies who want to make profits and don't want alternatives to their energy supplies.

Things are at last starting to change. We see wind turbines going up around the country. There are some hydroelectric schemes and tidal barrages being built. Some houses have solar panels fitted on their roofs. However, all of these measures are just scratching the surface and are still more expensive than burning fossil fuels.

MAIN POINT TWO: THERE ARE SOLUTIONS

Unfortunately, there has never been a solar cell made that makes more energy than it took to produce it. And all wind turbines are highly subsidized. But the problem of global warming and running out of fossil fuels has at least made people think about alternatives.

There is a project in Southern Spain where the sun's rays are captured by huge mirrors. The energy collected is used to make electricity. This produces electricity as cheaply as an oil fired power station and the scheme is likely to be expanded. Cover the Sahara desert in these solar power stations and Western Europe's energy needs are solved. Solar cells also produce virtually no carbon dioxide.

There is another project in a Scottish estuary where underwater turbines use the tide to produce cheap clean electricity.

However, the ultimate answer to our energy problems is to produce energy on the earth the same way as the sun. The sun uses a process we call *fusion* whereby atoms are *fused* together to make energy; hydrogen is converted to helium and vast amounts of energy are given off. Fusion is different to *fission* however. Fission is when we *split* an atom to make atomic bombs for instance - but there are lots of obvious problems and dangers with fission.

Research into *fusion* is going on all over the world. But the big problem we face is that the hydrogen must reach at least 15 billion degrees centigrade to start the process. So everything must be kept suspended in a magnetic field, because if we try to use a solid container, everything would start to melt and begin to cool down - and then the fusion process would stop.

So, it will be difficult to get fusion working but if the problems are solved fusion is the ultimate Get out of Jail Free card. It can produce as much energy as the world could ever need and the fuel source is hydrogen from seawater. It produces no pollution of any sort and will *not* increase global warming.

For example, if your car had a fusion engine then one cup of water would keep the car going *for your whole lifetime*; you would *never* have to buy any fuel again.

Let us hope that the energy problems of the world can be solved, because at the moment we have massive problems with energy usage.

SUMMARY

We've seen today, that the world faces big challenges. But challenges have been faced before and have been overcome. There have been world wars, there have been natural disasters. Now we are in a new world. A world in which energy is running out. But as we have seen in today's assembly, things *are* being done. We *can* rise to this challenge and win... *If* we all pull together.

CLOSING

Every one of you can help with the problems of energy usage and global warming. If every household in the country just turned one light off that is not needed, then we could close down a power station. If you all turn off devices that are not needed and don't leave equipment on standby you will not only help to reduce energy usage but will also save your parents' money.

Ask your parents how much their current electricity bill is. Ask them if you make a big effort to save electricity, and their next bill is reduced, can you have half of the money they have saved by you being careful. That would make you some extra pocket money and might just save the planet.

Thank you for listening.

Notes:

2

MAY DAY

AIM: To inform about this widely misunderstood occasion, this assembly gives an interesting historical overview.

OPENING HOOK

I wonder if anyone here does not know that we have a day off next week? I doubt it. I wonder if anyone here is not looking forward to it? I doubt it. I wonder if everyone here knows the reason why we have a day off next week? I doubt that too.

Well, next Monday you will all have a day off school to celebrate May Day. I wonder why? Has anyone got any ideas why this day should be a holiday?

Ask for ideas / discuss ideas with students. Generally there are a large number of different reasons suggested as to why we have a May day holiday.

I think we have had about (five) different reasons suggested as to why we have May Day celebrations, and you know what? Some of them may be correct - in one way or another.

May Day seems to have more causes associated with it than I have used red ink. And I've used a lot of that.

OVERVIEW

I'm going to look at all of the confused reasons why we're having a day off. And I hope you're all going to enjoy your day knowing something of its history. Do you know, May Day is something that has been celebrated all over the world for many, many years and for many, many reasons.

MAIN POINT ONE: RELIGION AND FERTILITY

The origins of this holiday go back a long way: May Day was considered to be the beginning of summer when the ground could be sown with seeds and eventually crops would be produced.

May day was celebrated in Egypt and India to worship the spring goddess. In Europe it has associations with the Celtic festival of Beltane (or Spring festival of fire); and with Walpurgis night in Germany (an alternative Halloween-type Spring celebration); and with many other Pagan celebrations.

As Christianity came to Europe the missionaries tried to ban all of the old pagan traditions. So May Day became associated with witchcraft and the works of the devil. But this had nothing to do with the original Pagan celebration. Even under threat of persecution many wanted to continue the May Day celebrations.

To celebrate the first of May, a May pole was usually erected. This used to be made of a tree that was felled before dawn and dragged to the centre of the village. The branches would be sawn off and the pole decorated with flowers and ribbons.

People would dance around the Maypole wearing ribbons, the hope being that during the dancing your ribbon may get entangled with someone for whom you have a love interest. So the celebration was not just about the fertility of crops.

This tradition also led to some attempts to ban May Day in the 17th century. The Puritans – who were a very strict religious group – felt that May Day had become a day of reckless sexual behaviour.

MAIN POINT TWO – WORKERS' RIGHTS

Later, May Day lost some of its associations with agriculture; it became a day when all social classes could mix together. Usually the Lord of the Manor, the clergy and land owners lived separate lives from those that worked in the fields. Naturally when they mixed together on May Day there was some social tension between those that were in charge and those that worked for them. The tensions between the classes could often result in fights breaking out especially as many had been celebrating by drinking alcohol all day.

This was the first time that May Day became associated with workers unrest, and the class divide between the have's and the have-not's.

May Day became further associated with civil unrest and workers rights in America during the 1880's. American workers had gone on strike to try to get an eight-hour working day. At the time people would often be told to work twelve or even fourteen hours a day for no extra pay whatsoever.

Eighty thousand workers went on strike in Chicago on May 1st 1880. This closed down most of Chicago's manufacturing industry.

After two days of striking a crowd gathered outside a factory in the Haymarket district. As the crowd surged forward several shots rang out; the police had fired into them killing four and wounding several others. The next day a bomb exploded killing a police officer. The police arrested some of the trade union leaders and they were hanged.

There was virtually no evidence that the people arrested had been in any way responsible for the bomb.

The Red Flag has been used by workers' movements since that day to honour the Haymarket martyrs and others who have shed blood in the battle for better working conditions.

May Day is still used as a time for protesting. If you check the news next Monday you will probably see people demonstrating on the street - somewhere in the world - against the government, capitalism or globalization.

In Iran, May Day celebrations have been banned because people were using it as a means of complaining about the way the country is being run. Workers have even been banned from having a picnic in the park.

SUMMARY

Well, we have gone from Pagan Gods to global capitalism in an effort to explain the origins of May Day. But what is probably most important about May Day today, is that it gives us an opportunity to peacefully protest. Living in a democracy gives everyone the chance to speak out about things they do not like, and May Day is just one of the ways we have of doing just that. So feel free to get our your red flags and marching boots, and get out there!

CLOSING

Or, if you don't feel like protesting, you could just enjoy your day off. At least now you know why you've got it!

3

NOBEL PRIZES

AIM: To inspire and inform, this assembly explains the surprising origin and purpose of Nobel's prizes

OPENING HOOK

Can anyone tell me what the following people all have in common:

- Marie Curie?
- Albert Einstein?
- Barrack Obahma?
- Martin Luther King?

They have all won Nobel prizes. These prizes are given in recognition of the greatest human achievements in science, medicine, literature, economics and international peace efforts.

OVERVIEW

Today I would like to tell you who Mr Nobel was and why he created his prizes. This will give us some idea of the great things that people are capable of.

MAIN POINT ONE – BIOGRAPHY ALFRED NOBEL

Alfred Nobel was a Swedish scientist and industrialist who was born in Stockholm in 1833. He took out hundreds of new patents on things he invented. However, he was most famous for the creation of dynamite. This was a new and relatively safe way of storing nitroglycerine; a very powerful liquid explosive that was highly unstable. Many people died as a result of nitroglycerine exploding when it was not supposed to.

Although dynamite contained nitroglycerine, it was quite safe to carry around because it would not explode until required to. This saved hundreds, even thousands of lives in the areas of construction and quarrying where high explosives were frequently used.

Unfortunately, Alfred Nobel's research into making dynamite caused a huge explosion at his factory that killed 5 people including his own brother, Emil.

In 1888 Alfred Nobel was mistakenly thought to have died. The obituaries written about him in the newspapers described him as a 'bringer of death'; and how his discoveries could only be used in wars to kill more people. It was thought that his *only* interest was in making more powerful explosives.

Alfred was devastated when he read this, as he felt his explosives could only bring good to the world by being used in mining and construction. He was a pacifist – pacifists believe that violence is always wrong and won't use it – and he did not believe anyone would consider using his inventions to kill people.

Nobel decided at this point to re-write his will. He left most of his wealth to the establishment of prizes. Nobel Prizes. His fortune has been invested ever since and the interest earned provides the money for prizes in physics, chemistry, medicine, literature, and for the promotion of peace. These consist of a medal, a personal diploma and a large cash award.

MAIN POINT TWO – PRIZE WINNERS

There have been approximately 540 Nobel Prizes awarded between 1901 and 2010. Only 41 of these have been awarded to women. Although in the modern world, that is sure to change.

In October 2009 Google had a doodle consisting of just a bar code. This was to celebrate the invention of charged-coupled devices. These are used in every digital camera and to produce images from the Hubble space telescope. Without them we would not have bar-code readers or modern medical-imaging technology.

These charge-coupled devices were developed by Charles Kuen Kao, George Smith and Willard Boyle. These three people all won the Nobel prize for Physics in 2009. But Nobel prizes are not just awarded for obscure ideas in Science that no one has ever heard of.

The social effects on our world, and the discoveries made by Nobel Prize winners often affect us all. After all, where would we be without our civil rights, or without our mobile-phone cameras?

SUMMARY

We have seen that this great prize came about because one man saw that each of us has the potential to do great good in this world, as well as great harm. And the emphasis here is on 'great'. Dynamite is a hugely destructive force for example, but it can also be used for great good in the areas of mining and construction. Nobel saw the need for people to achieve the *best* they can in a *constructive* way.

CLOSING

To win a Nobel Prize means a person has made a great contribution to the world. We have prizes and awards in our school, too. Because people who do well *should* be recognized. The Nobel Prize is the ultimate recognition. Who knows, maybe we have a future winner with us in the hall right now.

Notes:

4

FILE SHARING

AIM: This assembly is about file sharing, and the rights and wrongs of downloading information from the internet. Showing how easy it is to break the law without realising it.

HOOK

Are you a criminal - or are you sitting next to a criminal?

I am certain that the answer to this question is no, but do you ever share files of music or video with others on the internet?

Do you have a way of recording television programmes, and if so have you ever kept them for more than 6 months?

Have you ever read an article in a newspaper on sale in a shop, and then *not* bought the newspaper?

If your answer is 'yes' to any of these, then technically you are a criminal; you have infringed upon someone else's copyright. Recording a television program is not illegal of course, but keeping the recording for more than 6 months is, technically a crime.

OVERVIEW

It is file sharing in particular I want to talk to you about today; about how easy it is to just download a file without a thought, listen to the music or watch the film, and *not* pay anything for it.

I want you to consider the arguments for and against file sharing, and then decide if you think it is right or wrong.

Before I give any details I would like to take a vote. I am going to ask you three questions and I would like each of you to raise your hand for just *one* of the answers, then, at the end of the assembly I will ask the same questions again, and see if any of you have changed your minds.

There are moral issues at play here, because people everywhere are sharing files with thousands of others, most of whom they do not even know - right? So, the three questions I have for you are:

1. Who thinks free file sharing is okay; that it's just like lending a friend a CD or DVD. After all, if you're already in possession of the thing why not share it with your friends, right?

2. Who feels free file sharing is wrong; that you shouldn't lend out something to others if it actually belongs to someone else, or, if you do not *fully* own it yourself?

3. Who is undecided?

Can we have a show of hands on each of these questions now?

Well, it will be interesting to see if your views have changed by the end of the assembly.

MAIN POINT ONE – THE ARGUMENTS FOR AND AGAINST FILE SHARING

Not paying for a paper you have read the front page of on a news stand is technically illegal, but no one is likely to prosecute you, because reading a part of the paper encourages most people to buy the whole thing. In fact, this sort of 'free' information sharing is a commonly-recognised form of marketing books and magazines.

File sharing on the internet is however a major concern. If you get the music you want without paying, then those who make and distribute it get no money, so eventually there will be no more people making music. There is little point in being a musician or filmmaker if no one is going to pay you any money for what you have made.

On the other hand, some artists actually want people to file-share when they are new on the scene, because it gets their name about; just like reading front pages at the newsstand. Free advertising! For example, Radio Head released one of their albums free on the internet and just asked people to pay what they thought it was worth.

When radio first started playing music, people said it would be a disaster because everyone would stop buying gramophone records.

In the 1970's the invention of the cassette recorder meant teenagers could record music from each other and swap cassettes. Again there was a huge panic from retailers that everyone would stop buying vinyl records. In fact it is still 'illegal' to copy from cassette to cassette, but as far as I know no-one has ever been prosecuted for it.

File sharing online is different. It does not make a poor quality copy of the original. It actually makes a clone of the original; a perfect copy so there is little or no incentive to buy the real 'original' thing.

What should be done about this problem? Should those who file share be banned from the internet? Should they be prosecuted, fined or even put in prison? But there are often 5 million people or more file-sharing at any one time, so it may be quite expensive to build all the necessary prisons.

I have been looking at some blogs about file sharing and here are some of the reasons I found for why people think it is okay to do it.

1) A CD only has a few good songs. Most of the album is filler, so why should I buy the whole thing? Instead I can just download the songs I like.

2) CD's cost far too much. The five biggest music companies were sued for price fixing.

3) Even when one of the companies lowered its prices, they still would not print on the case the recommended retail price.

4) Music these days is terrible, that is why sales are declining. A 2006 poll of 18 to 34 year-olds say that music is getting worse.

5) I already own the tune on record or cassette so why should I not download a backup copy from the internet?

6) Taping off the radio is okay, so why shouldn't I download music files from the internet?

After hearing these points how many of you agree, and think it is reasonable to download music and other media from the internet without paying? Please put your hand up so I can count the votes.

Well, that is interesting. Here are a few points from the other side of the debate

1) If you download music without paying for it you are committing a criminal offence; just because music is not a physical thing does not mean it cannot be stolen.

2) Music is worth money and many CD's are reasonably priced.

3) Just because teenagers have limited budgets, doesn't mean it justifies stealing.

4) Trading MP3's is just like stealing from a CD shop.

5) The recording industry is suffering a massive decline in sales; so much so that they no longer make a viable profit from recorded music. The only profitable area at the moment is live performances and this will not be enough to support the entire music industry.

6) If something is not done, then you will no longer have music made by your favourite artists, because they will not bother to record music if no one is going to pay them for it. Would you be happy to have the next album by your favourite artist for free, but then have no more music produced by them in the future, because they have to go and earn money another way?

SUMMARY

After hearing the points for and against music piracy what is your view now? Has anyone changed their minds? Do you now think it is wrong to illegally download music? Please put your hands up if you now think it is wrong to illegally download.

I hope this has made you think about the implications of new technology and the access it gives us to illegal material, and the moral questions and choices raised.

CLOSING

Just remember that no money for artists will eventually mean no more artists. I wonder how the world would be if people stopped making music, producing pictures or writing books?

Notes:

5

SUMMERHILL SCHOOL

AIM: To inform about Summerhill, and provoke thought about different ways of running an organization

OPENING

Do you enjoy attending lessons?
Would you like to *not* have to wear a uniform, or *never* to have to take an exam unless you wanted to?

OVERVIEW

Today I would like to talk to you about a school where you don't have to do any of these things. In fact the pupils are in charge just as much as the teachers. The pupils decide what the school rules should be.

The following is from Summerhill School website.

> *"All crimes, all hatreds, all wars can be reduced to unhappiness"* wrote A. S. Neill, founder of Summerhill School.

"Today, all over the world, education is moving towards more and more testing, more examinations and more qualifications. It seems to be a modern trend that assessment and qualification define education.

If society were to treat any other group of people the way it treats its children, it would be considered a violation of human rights. But for most of the world's children this is the normal expectation from parents, school and the society in which we live.

Today many educationalists and families are becoming uneasy with this restrictive environment. They are beginning to look for alternative answers to mainstream schooling.

One of these answers is democratic or 'free' schooling. Democracy is where all the people who are affected by laws or rules vote for what those rules should be. There are many models of democratic schools in all corners of the globe, from Israel to Japan, from New Zealand and Thailand to the United States."

MAIN POINT ONE -SUMMERHILL

The oldest and most famous of these schools is Summerhill, on the east coast of England.

Summerhill School was founded in 1921 at a time when the rights of individuals were less respected than they are today. Children were beaten in most homes at some time or another and discipline was the key word in child rearing. Through its self-government and freedom Summerhill has struggled for more than eighty years against pressures to conform, in order to give children the right to decide for themselves. The school is now a thriving democratic community, showing that children learn to be self-confident, tolerant and considerate when they are given space to be themselves.

Summerhill was set up by A S Neil in Leiston Suffolk. He believed in a different type of education for children where they could choose what they wished to learn or, whether or not they even went to lessons at all.

The school is run on a democratic basis. All students and teachers at Summerhill have one vote at a weekly meeting. These meetings make school rules and give out punishments to anyone who has broken the rules. For example the fine for smoking is five pounds. This rule was recently made by the pupils.

In one case the punishment for breaking a rule was *not being allowed* to attend a geography lesson!

All school councils have their origin from Summerhill School. However, Summerhill School Council actually does make all the decisions on how the school is run.

The following is taken from Wikipedia

"In addition to taking control of their own time, pupils can participate in the self-governing community of the school. School meetings are held three times a week, where pupils and staff alike have an equal voice in the decisions that affect their day-to-day lives, discussing issues and creating or changing school laws. The rules agreed at these meetings are wide ranging - from agreeing on acceptable bed times to making nudity allowed at the poolside. Meetings are also an opportunity for the community to vote on a course of action for unresolved conflicts, such as a fine for a theft (usually the fine consists of having to pay back the amount stolen)."

"At the start of each year pupils come in for the day and choose what lessons they wish to attend. They can sign up for as much or as little as they like. If they do not wish to attend any lessons and just play all day; that is up to them."

There are drop-in lessons available all day if pupils want to spend a small amount of time in class and then go off again. One to one lessons are available to those who are struggling.

The school does not follow the national curriculum except in the case of pupils who wish to take GCSE exams.

MAIN POINT TWO: THE FIGHT TO SURVIVE

In March 2000 OFSTED (office for standards in education) demanded changes in the way the school was run. They were particularly concerned about the fact that lessons were not compulsory. This was felt to have a negative effect on the children's education. If this did not change the school would be closed down.

Summerhill School decided to fight the closure notice. They felt that Summerhill was a different school, not a bad school. They wrote to past pupils and friends of the school to raise the money needed for a court case.

Donations poured in and there was massive public support for the school. The court case is thought to have cost about £130,000. The case was defended by Geoffrey Robertson QC, the world renowned human rights lawyer.

He talked about past pupils. How many of them have gone on to be very successful in their chosen fields; actors, authors and university lecturers to name but a few. Summerhill pupils actually gain results above the national average and that is *without* compulsory lessons.

Geoffrey Robinson QC eventually discovered that the school was on a 'to be watched list' which was why the school was being inspected so often. This was not a legal practice if the school was not informed. The DFE case collapsed and they made an agreement with Summerhill School.

A meeting of Summerhill pupils took place in the Royal Courts of Justice, probably the first democratic meting ever to take place in a Royal Court of Law.

Summerhill is now the most protected school in the world and future inspections must include people who have experience of the progressive education that Summerhill offers.

SUMMARY

So, all schools are definitely not the same. Summerhill, as we have seen, is a place where students make up the rules with teachers, and change them when they want. This was brought about because A.S. Neil believed that people work best when they are in charge of their own lives.

CLOSING

This story is all about being different. A.S Neil was someone who believed there is a *better* way to educate children than the standard school model. He felt children would be happier if they had some control over how the school was run. He created a different type of school. At the time the school was created the newspapers were outraged and called it, 'that dreadful school!'. The established view was that children should be forced to attend lessons and made to work hard by beating them with sticks.

Those in charge of society are often afraid of things that are new or different. I hope you can all be more open-minded when you are confronted by new or different ideas.

You are, after all, the next generation.

Notes:

6

TIME

AIM: To educate and provoke thought about a complex but fascinating subject

Suitable for the anniversary of Harrison's watch (1713) (2013) – it is 300 years since the invention of the watch) or New Year's Day – or any other time related event.

HOOK

If you could travel in time where would you go? Or should I say *when* would you go? I wonder how many of you are thinking that you would go into the past. Would you be in Ancient Rome, in the Middle Ages or in Victorian England? Or would you go to the future? I'm guessing that most of you would choose the future, when you think about all the possible changes and wonderful inventions that will make life marvellous. And your life would certainly be different if you went into the past. You'd notice lots of changes there too.

I wonder what time actually *is*, and will we ever be able to build a time machine?

Another question that's worth thinking about; is time finite? Did time begin at a certain point - and will it ever end?

OVERVIEW

Today I would like to talk to you about time, about the fascinating process of trying to work out what time actually *is*, and how to measure it? Hopefully, this won't take up too much of your – time!

Did you know there is nothing in the laws of physics that says time travel is impossible; in fact many reputable physicists feel that one day it will be possible to construct a time machine. We just don't have the technology at the moment.

MAIN POINT ONE: THERE ARE DIFFERENT WAYS OF MEASURING TIME

How do we measure time?

Well today, we use watches. But in the past people used candle clocks or water clocks, even large versions of egg-timers with sand running from one section to another. But none of these were very accurate. To measure time *really* accurately we must use a device called an atomic clock - this is really a clock that uses light to measure time very accurately.

So what is the date and time now?

The date is (today's date and year) only because here we take our dates from the birth of Jesus. In the Jewish calendar it is the year 5771 (AD 2011 Gregorian) Go to http://www.hebcal.com/converter/ to find the date today. The Chinese have a completely different system based on the phases of the moon. As a result, the Chinese New Year starts on a different day each year, like our Easter.

So we see that dates are decided a bit randomly, and depend chiefly on a person's religion, where they were born, or where they live. So is time 'real' - was there actually an original 'day one'?

Well, we could think of 'day one' as the time when the earth was first formed. Radioactive dating tells us that the earth is about 4.5

billion years old, formed about half a billion years *after* the sun was created from a swirling cloud of hydrogen. The sun is about half-way through its life at the moment, and has another 5 billion years to go before it swells up and vaporises the earth. What a lovely thought!

But the formation of the earth cannot be called 'day one' because the materials that made the earth existed long before it was formed. Those materials came from a star that exploded billions of years *before* the earth was even a twinkle in the universe's eye.

So where did the materials to make the stars come from?

Well, the universe started about 15 billion years ago in a huge explosion called 'the big bang'. This was not something exploding *into* the universe, but was the actual creation of the universe itself, the beginning of space and time. So technically this was 'day one' because before that point there was no space and no time as we understand these concepts today.

So technically, we could say that today is (insert relevant time and date) 15 billion years from the creation of the universe.

MAIN POINT TWO: WHAT IS TIME ANYWAY?

Well, we now know what *the* time is... but I would like you to think for a moment about what time *is*.

Any ideas? (possible discussion with pupils from the audience)

It was believed that time was constantly passing at the same rate for everyone everywhere in the universe. This was until 1925 when a chap called Albert Einstein developed his theory of relativity. This is one of the greatest scientific theories ever created. It has passed every test that has been applied to it with flying colours. It was this theory in fact, that led on to the creation of the atomic bomb.

One of the strangest things that the Theory of Relativity predicts is that time is *not* a constant. It passes at different rates in different situations. The faster you go, the more time slows down: and the stronger a gravitational field, the more time slows down.

The only way to measure time very accurately is by the use of an atomic clock. Einstein's theory has been tested by using atomic clocks. If one is placed at the top of a tall building and another is placed at the bottom then the one at the top will run faster than the one at the bottom. The gravity at the bottom of the building is stronger than that at the top, so it slows time down.

An atomic clock placed in an aeroplane will run more slowly than one left on the ground. The faster you go the more time slows down. And at the speed off light time stops entirely.

If one identical twin were to remain on earth while the other went on a long journey at close to the speed of light, and then returned to earth after a few years, then the twin that went on the journey would be *younger* than the one that stayed on the earth. Amazing, isn't it? This is why technically, the Apollo astronauts are actually slightly younger than they should be because of their journey to the moon.

Time also slows down for particles in accelerators at Cern in Switzerland. (explain further about Cern if required). The particles exist for far longer when travelling at close to the speed of light than they would if they were stationary.

Another thing about the theory of relativity is that it does *not* preclude time travel. In theory therefore, it is possible to use a black hole (an area in space with intense gravity) to create a sort of time machine. So if astronauts in a space ship could get to a black hole and use their powerful rockets to just orbit around it, then the immense gravity of the black hole would actually slow time down.

The time difference would depend on how close the space ship was to the centre of the black hole, and how long it remained in orbit. It could just orbit the black hole for one space-hour for instance, then return to earth and the astronauts would find that everyone they had known were dead, and they could meet their own grown-up grandchildren who would by then, look even *older* than the astronauts!

This is because the astronauts would only have aged one hour. For everyone on earth however, 100 years or more could have elapsed.

So we see it is theoretically possible to use a black hole to make a time machine to travel to the future. These are not just silly ideas from science-fiction novels, but are serious scientific theories proposed by well-respected scientists. Time really does travel at different rates in different situations and dimensions.

SUMMARY

We've seen today that time can be measured in very different ways and that understanding exactly what time is – well, that's not nearly as easy as it seems. But I rather like the idea that the faster you go, and the more you do, the more time you have.

CLOSING

How have *you* used your time so far? How *will* you use it in future?

I would like us all to think about the past year. Have we spent our time well? Is there anything you or I would do differently if we could go back in time?

We cannot build a time machine just yet, so you can't change the past. But perhaps we can learn from the mistakes we've made. Remember, a mistake is not a mistake if we learn from it. So think about the next 365 days and let's see if we can manage them better than the last 365 days.

You only have so many days left in your life, so please do try to use the time wisely.

Notes:

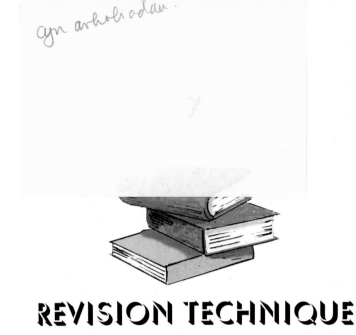

REVISION TECHNIQUE

AIM: To encourage effective methods of revising

HOOK

Good morning! You know, I am quite a lazy person. That is, I don't like doing more work than necessary to achieve a task. What about you? Do you like wasting your time? What about having to revise schoolwork when you would rather be doing something more enjoyable? So many students waste large amounts of time because they do not know how to revise properly, smartly or efficiently.

How many of you just read your notes and hope that it all goes in? Well, if you are one of those people you really are wasting your time.

Believe it or not, if you just read your notes, only about 4% is remembered, and you have no way of knowing if you can apply that knowledge to solving problems, or answering questions in an exam.

OVERVIEW

You can work much more efficiently if you revise smartly. And that's what we're going to be thinking about this morning. Smart ways of revising. Listen carefully, and I'm sure the information you're about to hear will make your school life a lot easier.

MAIN POINT ONE: THE USE OF KEY WORDS

Here's your first tip. Key words.

Read your notes, and find important key words and mark these out. For example, in the following passage I have identified seven key words that will be far easier to remember than the whole passage.

<u>(Present the key words on flash cards as you read the following)</u>

> *"To generate electricity we can use **fossil fuel** power stations. These **burn** the fuel to produce **heat**. This is used to produce **steam** which turns a **turbine**. This powers a **generator** which produces **electricity**."*

If we just learn the key words the overall context becomes apparent. Don't try to memorise it all.

Can you remember the overall context from the key words? <u>Show flash cards again.</u>

MAIN POINT TWO: CREATE YOUR OWN VISUALS

Here's another idea which is very similar to key words, in that it helps things stand out, and easier to remember.

Use pictures; images; posters; visuals. We often remember things we *see* better than things we hear about.

Make posters of those bits of information you usually forget, and place the posters on your bedroom walls. Cover up pop stars, footballers, whatever, and look at the posters every day.

This improves retention. That means it stays in your brain.

But the best technique is to use pattern diagrams. These are a special kind of visual aid.

First, start in the middle with the topic you are doing. The patterns you create link together the logical and creative sides of the brain. Obviously, using both sides of the brain is much more efficient.

Here is an example of a pattern diagram on energy.

<u>Presenter should draw the pattern on a board or use a projector.</u>

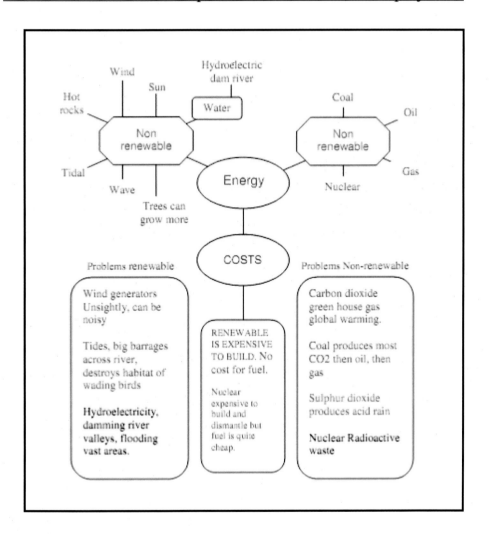

<u>From the title of Energy branch out with information about energy. Ask pupils what they could add to the diagram.</u>

Make it colourful, make it funny, perhaps even a little bit rude - these are the sort of things you remember.

Any areas you really struggle to remember; put a picture of someone you like such as Keira Knightly or David Beckham right next to the tricky area, and try to think of a mad connection between the two.

Place your finished diagram on the wall and look at for 10 minutes a day. Try some questions on the relevant area - and if you still cannot do them, just adapt the mind map as needed.

Once you have learnt the information, review the diagram after 2 days, one week, and one month. This will get the information into your long-term memory.

Eventually you will have lots of posters on your bedroom wall covering all the topics you need to know about.

MAIN POINT THREE: TAKE BREAKS

If you are doing GCSE or A-level work, recent research has shown that doing lots of exam papers is the best way to learn. If you cannot answer a question, get the correct answer from your teacher or answer schemes. Make sure you know how the problem is done. Then do it again. Keep reviewing by doing more pattern diagrams on different topics; all should go on a wall. Take a break after 20 minutes. Otherwise the percentage of information you remember rapidly drops off. If you take regular breaks, then the information stored rises up to its previous level. However, this is not a break to play seven missions on your computer game, but just 5 minutes relaxing looking out of the window having a cup of tea, giving your brain time to recover. Your brain uses sugar and gets tired like anything else. Do your revision in small chunks, don't try six hours of solid revision. Take breaks, have some time to yourself.

Once you think you've absorbed what you need to, have a go at some of the questions in your books under exam conditions. Try working with a friend and testing each other; ask for help from your friends or teachers if there are questions you still cannot answer.

MAIN POINT FOUR: TOP TIPS

- Plan your schedule with a revision timetable and stick to it.

- Try the BBC revision site 'bitesize' - an excellent resource.

- Some people can listen to music while revising, whereby the music gets associated with the topic. It is even possible to combine work and music by making up a song about the subject you are revising. There are lots of examples of this on the internet. Just put 'revision songs' and the topic you are revising into Google. Learn the song and the tune and this will help you remember the information. Again, you are associating the creative and logical sides of the brain. As an example possibly play *The Galaxy Song* by Monty Python as a way of revising the solar system and space.

- Before an exam, drink plenty of water so you are not dehydrated. Eat a banana for a slow release of energy; and go to bed early. If you cannot sleep then do some exercise at the gym or go for a run the night before an exam. Being physically tired will help you get a good night's sleep

SUMMARY

We have seen today that there are a lot of different ways of making revision easier: using key words, visuals, taking breaks, asking for advice, and more. Using these techniques will improve your exam results and requires less effort from you.

The time for revision is now.

CLOSING

I won't keep you any longer in this assembly. Please go and do some smart revision.

Notes:

8

DECISIONS, DECISIONS

AIM: To explore the way various choices are made and the impact those choices have on the world around us

<u>HOOK</u>

(<u>Ask audience</u>) Would you like a cream cake, or a mud-cake?

An easy choice, right? Every one knows that 'choice' means choosing. But some choices are really easy, while others can be very complicated, and we are all faced with many choices - some more important than others - as we go through life.

So what makes some choices easy, and others more difficult?

<u>OVERVIEW</u>

Let's take a look at some easy choices first:

Would you like a doughnut, or a chocolate cake?

Or; do you want the blue t-shirt, or the red one?

These choices are simple because they only involve *one* person, choosing between *two* options, with no obvious negative repercussions arising from the choices. So it only affects *you*.

Choices become far more difficult however when more than one person is involved in the decision-making, or, when other people can be affected by your choices.

For example, the choosing-a-cake decision becomes far less clear when you know your friend would like the same cake as you. Do you still take the cake you really want? Or, do you set aside your first choice in order to stay on good terms with your friend?

Or; how about choosing a classmate to be in your team? Is it more important to choose people who will win the game? Or, should you also consider people's feelings when they feel they are being overlooked - especially if they are your personal friends?

Unfortunately, most choices in life are not simply about doing what *we feel like* all the time. We also have to consider the options, the likely effects on other people, and any other possible repercussions. Most importantly perhaps, we need to take into consideration what is 'right' and what is 'wrong'. But it's rarely a simple choice.

OVERVIEW – MAKING MORAL CHOICES

As you go through life, you will constantly find yourself having to decide which is the 'right' or the 'wrong' decision to make, and there can be many factors that influence what you may think is 'right' or 'wrong' in any given situation. This is what we mean when we talk about making *moral* choices, and it is generally understood that good people will always try to make the right moral choices.

But sometimes you find yourself in a situation where choices you don't agree with are being made for you. Such as when the government declares war on another country; or when local councils bring in some new regulations. Adults at least, have a chance to alter things by voting at election time, but you have no immediate choice, do you? That's why it is important to make the right choices whenever you get the opportunity, and although you may sometimes regret some of the choices you make - as long as you *try* to make the moral choice - (at least as best you understand it) - then you can be confident that you are generally going in the right direction in life.

Unfortunately, moral choices can often be the most difficult to make.

MAIN POINT ONE: AN EXAMPLE OF A MORAL CHOICE

Here are some situations where we can take the easy choice, or the moral choice. Have a look at these decisions and choose the one you would make, (be honest) or, suggest a different choice altogether.

One of your friends has broken a rule but another friend is being blamed for it. Hands up if you would;

    a) Think 'hard luck for them - this is none of my business,' ..and do nothing at all?

    b) Speak to the friend who actually broke the rule and try to persuade him/her to own up?

    c) Tell the person in charge what actually happened?

Interesting, isn't it - especially when we have to think about the repercussions for ourselves and others. Should this affect our decision - or should we still 'do the right thing' anyway?

MAIN POINT TWO: A SECOND EXAMPLE

So we see, moral choices are not easy. Here's another example: You see a gang of people you know, attacking an elderly woman;

    d) Would you immediately go to help her - despite the danger?

    e) Would you use your mobile phone to call the police and be prepared to be a witness?

    f) Would you walk by and hope the gang doesn't notice you?

    g) Make an anonymous phone call identifying the gang?

In this case, making a moral choice could have very dangerous consequences for you. So do you do the 'right' thing - or is it okay to put morality aside when we need to look after our own interests?

Making moral choices often requires courage, especially when family and friends have different opinions to you. But ultimately, *you* are responsible for the decisions you make in life, and the decisions you make almost always affects others in some way.

MAIN POINT THREE: HOW TO MAKE THE RIGHT CHOICE

Here's a way of looking at it:

- First; be sure you have all the facts straight.
- Second; think about all of the people who may be affected by your choice.
- Third; think about what will probably happen after you have done whatever you think is right.
- Fourth; where possible, take advice from someone you trust.
- Finally; with everything taken into consideration, try to make the right *moral* choice - and be ready to stand by your decision.

SUMMARY

We have seen that not all choices are the same, and that not all decisions are easy. We have seen that the choices we make often affect others and that decisions about what is right, and what is wrong, are called *moral* decisions.

CLOSING

No one said that being a human is easy. Just remember that the decisions you make will help to shape the world for you and for others.

So think carefully. And always try your best to do the right thing.

9

DRUGS

AIM: To explain some of the effects of illegal drugs and discourage abuse

HOOK

Imagine you are really thirsty: no, not just thirsty but *really*, really thirsty! It is a very hot sunny day and you have been doing sport, then you eat some salt by mistake - which makes you even more thirsty. You go to get some water and there is nothing in the tap. You are absolutely desperate to have a drink but wherever you go there is no water. And your thirst is getting worse by the minute!

Just think about that for a moment.

Now imagine that someone has a cool bottle of water but they will not give you any, unless you pay them lots and lots of money.

That's what people say it is like to be addicted to drugs. Unfortunately, the craving for drugs is far, far worse than simply being very, very thirsty.

This is what drug dealers do. They get people addicted to substances so they feel they can't survive without them, and then charge them huge amounts of money to 'quench their thirst', that is; take the drug.

But within a day or two the drug addict is coming back for more; and the dealer charges the drug addict an even higher price. By now the addict will do *anything* to get hold of the drug; they will steal, use violence, go into prostitution or even murder people in some cases - *anything, anything* to get the next dose.

How does this happen to people? Well obviously, just like we see in the movies, there must be some shifty character out there driving a big black Mercedes trying to convince people to take drugs. If someone came up to you in the street and said, "hey do you want to try some drugs?" you would of course say 'No!' But it doesn't often happen like that, does it? The stereotyped image of drug dealers that we get from films is not really what they look like in real life - is it?

OVERVIEW

As young people, it's especially important to think about this problem, because you are particularly vulnerable. We need to understand how this happens; how is it that so many very 'normal' people find themselves getting addicted. And how it is that so many young people, full of life, and full of potential, end up ruining their lives before they have even properly begun.

MAIN POINT ONE: HOW ADDICTION CAN START

In fact you could be sitting next to a drug dealer now - have a look at the person sitting next to you - are they a drug dealer? Well no, of course they're not. But the fact is that most people who get addicted to drugs were offered them for the first time *by friends*.

I wonder what sort of friends *they* were?

Have any of your friends offered you drugs?

Before you say 'No' - just ask yourself if a friend has ever offered you some alcohol to drink, or a cigarette?

These are drugs too. They may be 'legal' drugs in Britain, but they are drugs all the same, and it is *illegal* for you to take them if you are under 18 years of age.

A drug is anything that alters your state of mind. This includes certain medicines of course, including painkillers and sleeping tablets. But any medicines that might be dangerous are strictly controlled by the government and the medical profession. They are *legal* if a doctor prescribes them, but *illegal* if you get them from someone else. And if they are *illegal*, you may be sure that they are dangerous as well.

Drugs that are *illegal* are usually taken for the first time at a party. No, not the type of party where the guy in the black Mercedes is lurking in the shadows, but a normal party where people are simply enjoying themselves; maybe they have had too much to drink and one of their friends says, "Hey do you want to try some of this? It'll make you feel great!"

And of course, drugs *do* make you feel great - at least for a short time - otherwise no one would take them. But it's the *long-term* effects that people aren't so eager to talk about.

Some drugs are addictive only after they have been taken a few times; others, like crack cocaine, are instantly addictive.

You need to ask yourself why someone would want to make *me* feel so good? The reason is usually because they want to make money out of you, by getting you addicted to the drug. If they use drugs too, then you can be sure that *your* money goes to support *their* habit.

MAIN POINT TWO: HEALTH DANGERS

Drugs are not only addictive but are very bad for your health.

Drugs can cause mental illness - severe damage to the liver, kidneys and heart. They can destroy your veins and cause premature aging. They could make you look 50 years of age when you are still only a teenager and they will, of course, eventually kill you.

Dealers often dilute the drugs with toilet cleaner or bird droppings, so they can have more for themselves. And I'm sure I don't have to tell you that toilet cleaners and bird droppings are not the best things to be circulating in your bloodstream either - right?

SUMMARY

We have seen today that addiction is a terrible thing – once you are hooked, it's very hard to go back. We have also seen that addiction to drugs makes people do awful, selfish and hurtful things. Likewise, the people who sell drugs do not care about you at all. They only care about themselves, and don't care how many lives they destroy as long as they can make more money. Is this really the sort of person you need in your life?

CLOSING

You are all wonderful young people and life is only just beginning for you. The real 'drug' in life is staying happy, alert and full of life, and using all of your faculties to enjoy the adventure of growing up in a fascinating world that is so full of promise.

I can safely say I have had far more fun since I left school than I had while I was there. So trust me; you don't need drugs to enjoy life. In fact, taking drugs is the surest, quickest way to ruin your life.

So please think carefully, and if ever you're asked at a party, 'Wanna try some of this?' - you now know what the answer should be.

10

ANGER

AIM: To foster anger management, this assembly looks at different strategies for controlling one's temper

HOOK

I am so angry, I'm so very, very angry. You know why? You *really* want to know why? I'll tell you why at the end of assembly!

OVERVIEW

This assembly is about anger. We're going to be looking at the causes, the dangers, and above all how to deal with it. Anger *can* sometimes be appropriate, after all, some things are so very annoying aren't they? But losing your temper, or reacting purely out of anger is rarely a good thing. Sometimes, being angry over something leads to a *good* decision being made, but even in such cases, decisions are best left until *after* the anger clears.

MAIN POINT ONE: SOME OF THE CAUSES

What are the causes of personal anger? Here are some of them:

- Feeling insulted
- Being passed over
- Taking offence at an idle remark
- Being bullied
- Being accused unjustly

Ask for more suggestions and situations which have made members of your audience feel angry. Discuss these.

MAIN POINT TWO: STRATEGIES

If you give yourself time to think before responding in anger – perhaps by counting to ten – it could help to diffuse the situation before things get worse.

The bible tells us that, "a soft answer turneth away wrath." It also helps to confuse the person who is feeling angry with you because they are probably expecting you to make an angry reply.

Role Play – have two students or teachers already briefed on this.

Accuser – Why did you tell my friend I said nasty things about her?

Accused – Well you did, didn't you.

Accuser – No I didn't, you're just a trouble maker.

Accused – No I'm not, she's *my* friend too, and she's not *your* friend any longer, so there!

How are they both feeling now? Both quite angry perhaps?

Here's another way of dealing with the situation:

<u>Accuser</u> – Why did you tell my friend I said nasty things about her?

<u>Accused</u> – All I said was you'd noticed a hole in her pullover.

<u>Accuser</u> – Well she said you were nasty about it.

<u>Accused</u> – I'm sorry she thought that. There was no offence intended. I was in a hurry and told her as I walked past her. I didn't think I'd upset her, and I'll apologise to her when I see her again.

So, are they both feeling angry now? What's the difference?

SUMMARY

We have seen how quickly anger can arise and we have seen that responding defensively or angrily, without thinking, can be a big mistake. Take the time to reflect before responding.

CLOSING

Many years ago my grandmother gave me some very useful advice. She said, 'Don't ever take offence. It doesn't matter what anyone says, just don't take offence, because if you *know* you have done nothing wrong, you cannot be hurt.'

Keep calm, and explain your point of view, but listen to the other person and try to imagine why they are angry.

So next time you feel angry, take time to count to ten *very* slowly before you speak.

I said at the beginning that I was very angry and I was going to tell you exactly why. Well, having had time to think about it and count to ten, I don't feel angry at all now!

Notes:

11

THE DANGERS OF ALCOHOL

AIM: To encourage restraint in drinking, this assembly gives some of the sobering facts…

HOOK

I want to talk to you today about a very serious matter. It's something shocking and it's something which has been going on for a very long time. And in one way or another it already affects everyone, and *will* affect everyone in this room.

When you or your friends deliberately take a substance which you know will change your mood, and you know will change the way you think, you are of course taking a huge risk. Because if you lose control of your mind, even for a short while, you may do things that change your life forever; that your life will never be the same again. It might even destroy you. Or, destroy people around you. OR both.

The substance we are talking about causes long term damage to our health, including 10% of all ill health and early deaths in Europe.

IN the UK in 2006 this substance caused 8,386 people to die young. 8,386! There are around (1000) people in this hall. Eight times that number died unnecessarily young. You cannot pick up a newspaper without reading stories of lives ruined by the horrors of this substance. And the scary part is that it's not even illegal!

OVERVIEW

So, what are we talking about? We're talking about alcohol of course: beer, wine, spirits, cider. It's an issue which needs to be taken very seriously, and that's what I want to do today.

MAIN POINT ONE: EXPLORING A GOVERNMENT ADVERTISING CAMPAIGN ON THE SUBJECT

An advertising campaign on television recently, is trying to make people think about what they are getting into if they drink too much alcohol. One advert features a young man, the other a young woman. In each case they are going out for the evening.

Before they leave the house, they wreck their clothes, they vomit on the carpet, they trash their personal belongings and they injure themselves. And the advert ends with the words – "You wouldn't start a night like this, so don't finish it like this!"

And here's the point. Alcohol – wine, beer, spirits – changed the way those characters thought, and changed their mood and behaviour to the point where they actually thought it didn't matter that they were slowly wrecking their lives. In fact, they thought it was fun.

Lets think about this advert for a moment and take it a bit further.

Let's imagine this scene over a lifetime. It is sad but it is true, that there are many people in their forties whose lives are already ruined.

You young people are just about to start out on your adult lives, and will no doubt be presented with the opportunity to drink. The question is, where will alcohol take *you*?

Girls, will you be a woman whose children despise you because you are never sober; will you embarrass them by not talking sense when their friends come round; will you not be able to dress them - or yourself - in the morning because you are so hung over? Girls, you wouldn't start your life like this. Don't finish it that way.

Boys, will you waste all your earnings; will you become a violent swearing bully; will your wife and children fear you - or be ashamed of you; will your liver fail, turning your face yellow as you desperately wait for a transplant in hospital? Boys, you wouldn't start your adult life like this. Don't finish it that way.

MAIN POINT TWO: AN APPROACH TO DRINKING

Now, I'm not saying never drink. That's probably not realistic. But you need to know *now* about the dangers. You need to think about this *now*, when you are just about to start out on your adult life.

Firstly, do not drink when *you* don't want to. And never let anyone make you think you should.

Second. If you do drink, do it slowly. And remember that some alcoholic drinks are much stronger that others. Know your limits.

Be aware: Alcoholic strength is measured by something called 'ABV'; 'alcohol by volume'. The average beer is about 4% ABV. If you drink beer with more than 4% ABV then you need to take special care because the dangers to yourself and others increase as the ABV percentage increases.

Wine is usually about 12% ABV, and so is much stronger than beer. You need to drink wine in much smaller quantities, and far more slowly than beer if you are to avoid potential problems.

Spirits, which includes vodka, whisky and gin are around 40% ABV. That is a massive percentage of alcohol. If you drink a lot of vodka in one straight session for instance, it could easily kill you, because ultimately, alcohol is a poison.

It's sad but true that many people in this city of ours have had their lives ruined by drink. Their minds, their health gone. Will you let that happen to you too?

SUMMARY

We have seen today some of the terrible things that can happen to people who let alcohol take over their lives. We have seen that it takes strength of character to deal with it.

CLOSING

There is a huge liver unit in a major hospital in most cities. They give transplants to people whose livers are ruined. Many don't make it. Too much drink.

You wouldn't want your adult life to finish that way - would you?

Then don't start it like that.

12

DUNKIRK

AIM: To educate about a dramatic part of history and encourage self-reliance

HOOK

There is always 'an atmosphere' when a large group of people are gathered together in one place. An atmosphere of tension, of anticipation: and the bigger the group, the bigger the atmosphere.

There are probably more than <u>one thousand</u> people in this hall now – <u>one thousand</u> people.

When you get a lot of people gathered together like this, you can be sure that there will be lots of differences between them: but also a lot of things in common. The subject I am going to talk about today is to do with something all <u>one thousand</u> of us have in common.

We are all living on an island – a big one, but an island all the same. Britain is surrounded by the sea. If, like us, you live in England, Scotland, Wales or Ireland then you cannot go to any other country without sailing across the sea or flying over the sea – or maybe, even swimming across the sea. But if you did swim then you would have to go 23 miles without stopping. We are surrounded by the sea – we are an island race.

Now not many countries are like this. Very, very few big countries are islands: think of our nearest neighbour, France. A Frenchman or woman could cross how many countries without needing to swim? How many countries could you walk to directly? Belgium, Luxembourg, Germany, Switzerland, Italy and Spain – that's six. But then of course, you could keep walking all the way to China if you wanted to, and never have to get your feet wet.

But you can't do that if you are British.

Being surrounded by water has been an important part of the history of this country.

We became very good at sailing, so much so that they made up a song about it – "Rule Britannia! Britannia rules the waves".

So many times the sea has saved us. Saved us from the threat of invasion. You may have heard of the Emperor Napoleon? 200 years ago he wanted to attack England from France. He had 130,000 soldiers ready to cross the English Channel and make us all speak French. But he didn't. You know why? He couldn't risk crossing the water. His soldiers couldn't swim 23 miles (especially in all that armour) and his navy would have been beaten by the British navy anyway - and he knew it. So he backed off.

One hundred and thirty thousand – that was an awful lot of soldiers when you think about the <u>one thousand</u> students we have in here. I thought <u>one thousand</u> was a lot – but one hundred and thirty thousand!

OVERVIEW

There was a time in more recent history when an even greater number of men were gathered on the beaches of Northern France. In fact it is about 70 years ago that a huge group of men were gathered on the beach in Northern France. That place was Dunkirk. We're going to hear about one of the greatest escapes of all time. An entire army rescued from captivity at best, and at worst, annihilation and sudden, horrible deaths for tens of thousands of soldiers.

MAIN POINT ONE: THE DUNKIRK TRAP

This group of men were soldiers again, only this time they were British soldiers. It was May 1940. We had declared war against Germany in 1939. And why wouldn't we? Germany was ruled by the Nazis; the most evil group of people known to man; the most racist; the most ruthless; the most frightening.

Unfortunately, not only were they very evil, they were also very clever – which is not a good combination, especially if you're on the other side. Being so evil and so clever had meant they had built up the most powerful and frightening army the world had ever known.

So we went to France to fight them. Well, we got a big shock because we could not beat them. They were so powerful. We did the only thing we could – we ran. We ran back through France. Back and back we ran until we could run no further, because we had arrived at the sea and we could not run through that - nor swim the 23 miles home. And there simply were not enough ships to save us.

You know how many men were stuck on that beach at Dunkirk being chased by the Germans with their machine guns, their tanks and, worst of all, the fighter planes and bombers?

Well, not <u>one thousand</u> like the number of people here now. Not 130,000 like Napoleon had. No, there were *one hundred and thirty eight thousand men* expecting to be caught or killed by the Nazis.

Churchill told his MP's to prepare to tell the country 'the worst news ever'. He told them to get ready to tell the British people of the terrible tragedy that he believed was about to happen. But the tragedy didn't happen as anticipated. Because you see, we didn't give up.

MAIN POINT TWO: THE ESCAPE

Winston Churchill told his commanders to try to save the army, even though it seemed impossible. This last-ditch rescue effort was known as 'Operation Dynamo'.

And so all the Royal Navy ships that could get there, went there – but not only that: If you had gone to the seaside in May 1940 you would have noticed something missing – the commercial fishing boats; the pleasure boats; the dinghies; the yachts; even the rowing boats for goodness' sake. For everyone who owned a boat, no matter how small, no matter how old, battered and leaking, had gone to Dunkirk. If you had a piece of wood that floated, you took it across the Channel to help.

SUMMARY

All those soldiers on the beach at Dunkirk had been expecting the Nazis to arrive at any moment. But instead of German tanks and bombers coming to get them, it was a flotilla of English boats that came over the horizon. They got there first. And because of their guts and determination, the army was saved to fight another day.

CLOSING

What can we learn from this? It seems to me to be summed up in the words of an old song.

"When the going gets tough, the tough get going!"

Or, as Winston Churchill himself said,

"When you're going through Hell – keep going!"

13

DYSLEXIA

DYSLEXIA

AIM: To heighten awareness and understanding of dyslexia

HOOK

What do you think the following people all have in common?

Alexander Graham Bell , Thomas Edison, Albert Einstein, Leonardo da Vinci, Pablo Picasso, George Washington, Agatha Christie, Richard Branson, Jay Leno, Vince Vaughn, Whoopi Goldberg, Bill Gates, Tom Cruise, Kiera Knightly, Orlando Bloom and world champion boxer Muhammad Ali.

All of the above were or are Dyslexic.

OVERVIEW

I want to look at the nature of this condition; I want to understand it a bit better, and I want you to come on this journey with me.

MAIN POINT ONE: A DEFINITION

Most of you in the audience have probably heard about dyslexia, and some of you might even be dyslexic, but very few of you probably know exactly what dyslexia is.

So it's probably best to begin this assembly with a basic description of what dyslexia is, and how it affects those who have it.

Dyslexia is defined as; *a specific reading disability due to a deficiency in the brain's processing of graphic symbols; a learning disability that alters the way the brain processes written material.*

Another definition says: *Dyslexia is not a disorder, disease, or biological error. It is a specifically designed brain with different strengths than a 'normal' brain.*

Although from the definitions it doesn't sound very glamorous or very useful, the benefits of the dyslexic condition are in fact vast, and many of those who have had this condition (some of whom I just mentioned) have made a lasting impact on our world in some way, and even gone down in history; although from a 'normal' perspective they were often considered to be 'at a disadvantage'.

MAIN POINT TWO: SUCCESS STORIES

However it could also be said that the so-called 'disadvantage' of having dyslexia could be one important reason why many of those people were, or are, so brilliant in their respective fields. It could be argued then, that without dyslexia we would not have had our Albert Einsteins, Leonardo Da Vincis, or our Bill Gates.

Some still believe that dyslexic brains are wired wrongly. But judging from some of the people previously mentioned you could argue that this so-called 'faulty wiring' seems more of a help than a hindrance, and that having dyslexia played a large part in their brilliance, and contributed directly into making them who they are.

Most people are not aware that people with dyslexia have some key benefits over those who do not have it: this includes being highly intuitive and insightful, being good at logic and spatial skills, and having the ability to think mainly in pictures, to name but a few.

Some might say that the benefits of being dyslexic do not make up for the other issues that dyslexics have to endure, including problems with spelling, punctuation and grammar.

But thinking back to our list of dyslexic people, it is obvious that the condition never stopped those like Bill Gates from founding Microsoft and creating the operating system Windows; it never stopped Einstein from changing our understanding of the universe forever with his theory of relativity; and it never stopped Thomas Edison from creating the light bulb and many other inventions, although, as with most dyslexics, they each struggled in school.

For instance; Albert Einstein's teachers said that he was, *"Mentally slow, unsociable, and adrift in his foolish dreams"*. Could it have been that it was those foolish dreams that paved the way for his ideas about the theory of relativity?

Another teacher sent a note home with a six year old Thomas Edison, saying, *"He is too stupid to learn"*.

Winston Churchill, one of the greatest political leaders to have ever lived, was continually punished in school for failure, or lack of effort, sometimes failing the same class numerous times.

SUMMARY

From the examples just given, you would never have thought that these people would turn out to change the course of history. Although these are just a few examples, they are not at all isolated. Others such as Vince Vaughn, Muhammad Ali and Jay Leno all got similar reports or had similar discouraging experiences in school.

Thankfully though, times have changed and our understanding of the dyslexic condition and many others like it, is better than ever before; allowing teachers to better provide for, and help students who are affected by dyslexia.

But it is still up to the individual to *choose* to put in the effort to overcome and, in some cases, work with the problems that a person with dyslexia faces. And as we've clearly seen, if you do decide to make the effort, the potential for achievement is unlimited.

CLOSING

So, if you are dyslexic and you find some things difficult that others don't, just remember you are part of an exclusive club that includes geniuses such as Einstein, De Vinci, and Edison; world class actors such as Tom Cruise, Keira Knightly and Orlando Bloom; famous writers and artists like Agatha Christie and Picasso, and highly successful businessmen such as Richard Branson. All of them belong to the same exclusive club.

So the next time you think dyslexia is a disability or disadvantage, just think again about the exclusivity of the club that dyslexic people belong to.

But those of us who are not dyslexic, and do not belong to this exclusive club of potentially world-changing geniuses, should also remember the various disadvantages that people with dyslexia have to endure, work with, and overcome, on a day-to-day basis.

14

GALILEO

AIM: To inform about Science Technology and the implications of new discoveries

HOOK

What is the hardest thing to understand? Maths? The opposite sex? Why Mr (name of teacher) can apparently never find a matching pair of socks in the morning?

Admittedly, all of these things are difficult to work out and maybe we'll never get to the bottom of them. But what about this: what if you set yourself the task of trying to work out the meaning of *everything*. Yes, *everything*. That's what you're doing when you try to work out what the universe is all about. And scientists have been trying to do it - and doing it with some measure of success - for many years now.

OVERVIEW

It must have started thousands of years ago; that first person looking up at the stars and wondering what it was all about, how it worked.

Today we're going to look at one of the greatest scientists of all time; how he started to work it out and how others built on what he started.

MAIN POINT ONE: GALILEO

It was approximately 400 years ago (25th of August 1609) that Galileo Galilei first demonstrated his new telescope. A small device that would change our understanding of the universe.

At the time it was believed that the earth was at the centre of the universe and all other heavenly bodies rotated around the earth.

It was believed that God had placed *us* at the centre of the universe because we were his creation. This *Geocentric* system was proposed by Aristotle in the fourth century.

Observations with Galileo's telescope showed that Jupiter had moons which rotated around Jupiter, *not* the earth. It also showed that the moon was not completely flat as had long been believed. The observation that Venus also went through phases like the moon was also a clear indication that the earth was not at the centre of the solar system after all.

The perfect circular orbits envisaged by Aristotle no longer matched the observations. This upset Church leaders, who then threatened to torture Galileo to death if he did not recant his discoveries (to state publicly that what he had published was wrong).

He *did* recant under threat of torture, but still spent the final decade of his life under house arrest. He knew his observations showed that the earth moved around the sun and was therefore *not* stationary at the centre of the universe as the church believed. This sun-centered (*heliocentric*) system had been proposed by Nicolas Copernicus at least 100 years before Galileo first used his telescope, but Copernicus too had been forced to suppress his discoveries because they clashed with prevailing religious beliefs.

The Church eventually changed its view about the solar system in 1757 when Pope Benedict XIV suspended the official Catholic Church ban on works that supported the heliocentric model.

MAIN POINT TWO: SOME SUBSEQUENT DEVELOPMENTS

In 1969 America landed a man on the moon. Space probes have now landed on nearly all the planets in our solar system, and satellites pepper outer space. We use satellite TV and satellite navigation on a daily basis.

We now have a very good understanding of the solar system in which we live. The moon is about a quarter of a million miles away from the earth and the sun is 93 million miles away. It is not possible to draw the distance to the planets to scale on a piece of paper as either the distance to Mercury is too small to be seen or, the paper would need to be several miles long.

The sun itself orbits around the centre of our Galaxy, which is called the Milky Way. The Milky Way contains at least 100 million stars. In the entire universe there are at least 1 billion galaxies.

It is difficult to comprehend these numbers. But I would like you to think about being on a beach picking up a handful of sand and counting how many grains of sand there are. How long do you think would that take? Then think about how many grains of sand there are on the entire beach. Now think about all the beaches in the world and count how many grains of sand there are on them. That is about the same as the number of stars in the universe. Our sun is just one of those stars.

Recent research has shown that most stars we have examined have planets orbiting around them. It is very very probable that there are planets out in space that have intelligent life living on them. We are far from being at the centre of the universe as was believed by the Church in the time of Galileo. In fact we live on the surface of a sphere of space-time, so really, the universe cannot have a centre.

In 1687 Sir Isaac Newton printed his Principia Mathematica. This highly influential work describes the physical laws that govern the universe. It was Newton's theory that enabled Man to land on the moon in 1969.

MAIN POINT THREE: WHERE IT HAS GOT US?

If Galileo and others had not been determined to find out how the world really works and, didn't have the courage to challenge the dogma of the time, then we really would still be in the dark ages. Without scientific discovery we would not have modern medicines, televisions, computers, planes, cars and all the other technology we take for granted.

SUMMARY

We've seen how scientific enquiry has opened up an understanding of space, and of the place of our world in the universe. We've seen how this knowledge can change our lives and the lives of those around us.

CLOSING

There are many things we *can* do that perhaps we *should not* do. Would it be right to create designer babies? It is already possible to select a fertilized egg that does not have abnormalities so that a baby will be healthy. Very soon it may well be possible to enhance embryos so that the child is highly intelligent, brilliant at music, taller, better looking or anything the parents want. Would you feel comfortable if this had been done to you?

There is always a balance between the discoveries of science that enable us to do many new things, and the ethical dilemmas that surround some of these discoveries. You will all be able to vote when you reach the age of 18 and different political parties have different views on all these issues.

But if you do not understand the issues and do not ask those difficult questions, then you cannot really make an informed decision about whom to vote for. This is really what education is all about.

So, be brave and inquisitive like Galileo and Copernicus; and don't be afraid to ask those difficult questions!

15

THE GUNPOWDER PLOT

AIM: To make history come alive and encourage tolerant thinking

HOOK

Sometimes I think you don't appreciate how lucky you are! No, that's not quite fair. Sometimes I *know* we *all* don't appreciate how lucky we are!

I don't know if you, like me, have ever enjoyed seeing a fabulous firework display? It's not just entertainment for children, is it? There is an amazing level of professionalism about most of these displays.

When I was young, the 5th November celebrations were a simple case of a small bonfire at the bottom of the garden, a few fireworks and maybe a sparkler or two.

Today, you're lucky!

But it's strange to think that the enjoyment we all get from firework displays today, only happens because of truly horrible things that happened many years ago.

One of the things we like about this school is how we take pride in, and relish our cultural diversity. That means that even though we live and work with people who are different from us, we are not suspicious of them, and we don't make enemies of them just because they are from a different race or religion. No, we celebrate and rejoice in our common humanity, and take pride in our joint purpose in making the school a successful happy community.

Unfortunately, the world in which we live is not always like this. And historically our own society was *certainly* not always like this.

OVERVIEW

In 1605, there were terrible hatreds and suspicions in this country of ours, and mainly it was about religion. I'd like to talk to you today about how these suspicions and hatreds led to real horror – for the events that led to bonfire night were truly horrible. And I'd like to think that each of you will help to build a society of respect and tolerance, where such hatreds really are a thing of the past.

MAIN POINT ONE: HISTORY OF NOVEMBER 5TH

Many of you will know from your history lessons, that many years ago Christianity split into two main groups: The Protestants and the Catholics. Feelings at the time ran so high, that most people thought that the country had to be either *all* Protestant, or *all* Catholic. They felt there could be no compromise or cooperation, because they simply couldn't envision living together.

Robert Catesby was a Catholic. He was a friend of Guy Fawkes. He had had enough. The King was not kind to Catholics. In fact it was more or less against the law to be a Catholic. You couldn't have a

Catholic priest come to your house for example. If you were caught harbouring a priest you could be heavily fined, tortured or even put in prison.

So Robert Catesby got a group of his Catholic friends together and said in so many words, "Let's Kill the King!" He then prepared a plan to blow up the Houses of Parliament along with the King, the royal family and the Members of Parliament - all at the same time.

So one night, just before the official opening of the Houses of Parliament, Catesby and his friends put 36 barrels of gunpowder underneath the very place the King would be sitting the following day. They left one man, Guy Fawkes, in the cellars with the gunpowder – whose job was to light the fuse in the morning. The others planned the getaway. They had horses ready on stand by. They were going to ride to the Midlands and hide there. They hoped that Spain, a Catholic country, would then invade England and turn it into a Catholic country, so that English Catholics could regain their liberties and bring an end to the unjust persecutions.

But someone had given the game away. Someone had as they say, 'grassed them up' and Guy Fawkes was caught in the cellar.

The King's men tried to find out the names of the other people who had been planning with him. The torture he suffered was terrible.

Eventually they found out what they wanted to know.

All of the plotters were caught. Some were killed in a shoot-out at one of their hideaways in the Midlands. They were the lucky ones. The others were burned to death in public. I would tell you of the tortures they suffered before they died but it's too harsh, too horrible.

The King thanked God he had been saved. He said that every year on November 5th the nation should celebrate and thank God. The country, he thought, should remember that 'evil people' who turn on the King will suffer and burn.

MAIN POINT TWO: TOLERANCE AND CELEBRATION OF CULTURAL HERITAGE

One of the many things we are proud of in this school is the way we can all get along together. And it's not just in this school. In Great Britain as a whole tremendous progress has been made in ensuring that people get along, and that we allow others to celebrate God – or not, if they prefer – in the way they believe. And no-one gets hassled about it, let alone tortured or killed. There is still work to be done of course. Not everyone yet thinks quite like this. But we are getting there.

SUMMARY

In summary, remember that terrible things have been done because people refused to allow others to have their own beliefs.

> Remember, remember, the fifth of November,
> ..and remember... we have all moved on.

CLOSING

So, yes, we are lucky. We need to think about how lucky we are.

Not just that we have fantastic firework displays to watch and enjoy on November 5th, but more importantly, that we now live in more civilized times. Times where we do not just 'put up with' or tolerate others being different from us.

We rejoice in it!

16

POSITIVE SELF IMAGE

AIM: To develop positive self-thoughts, this assembly encourages students to develop inner self confidence

HOOK

There are some things in this school which really annoy me, things that really get on my nerves!

I'm not a mind reader. But I know what you're thinking. There are things in this school that annoy you too. I might be one of them for all I know. I understand that. Teachers can indeed be irritating at times. Maybe it seems like we are always *demanding* things of you – to do your homework, tidy your uniform, stop talking in class, follow the school rules, etcetera.. It's true. We *do* demand a lot from you. But we also try to make sure we are not always criticizing you. Certainly, we try to make sure that we praise you too. We congratulate you for the good things you do, of which there are many. We tell you when you do well.

We believe in you. We believe you will continue to do the best you can, and maybe even achieve great things in life…

<u>OVERVIEW</u>

But do *you* believe in you? Do you really? Well, you should. Let's look at how you actually think about yourself.

Today, I am going to talk to you about some things which are quite personal to you. I'm not going to ask anyone to tell us their private thoughts, but I am going to ask you to think about some very personal things.

<u>MAIN POINT ONE: LISTEN TO THE VOICE IN YOUR HEAD</u>

Here's the first one. I said that teachers are often telling you what to do. But we try not to criticize you as a person. It would be wrong to do that because we believe in you - in your potential.

But think.

Is there anyone who criticizes you all the time, anyone who really nags you, gets to you, makes personal attacks on you as a person - *all* the time?

Think about that. The real answer may be surprising. Sometimes the person who has a go at you is very close. Closer than you think perhaps?

I said I was going to ask you to think about something, but just for a moment let's do the opposite. Don't think about anything - nothing at all - stop thinking.

Can't do it?

That's because we always think. We're human, and when we think, it's in the form of a voice, isn't it? Listen to it - that voice in your head. Whose voice do you hear?

Well, it's *your* voice, isn't it?

MAIN POINT TWO: CONTROL THE VOICE IN YOUR HEAD

Now, try this experiment for me. Think of someone you like who is confident, maybe a lot more confident than you, someone who is happy, enthusiastic and confident.

Now, think *your* thoughts in *their* voice.

Easy, isn't it?

You see, you control the voice in your head. You can make it change. Too often, people give themselves a hard time. That voice in their head tells them off. Tells them they are no good. Sometimes your own voice in your head tells you negative things about yourself. Your own voice may say things to you like: 'I knew I'd get that wrong; I am useless; why am I always so stupid. Nobody likes me. I'm not good at anything!'

SUMMARY

Why do you let that voice keep having a go at you? After all, it's *your* voice and *you* control it.

Next time your internal voice tells you that you are *not* a good person, tell it to shut up!

Tell it to say something nice about you. Do it now. Think about something you are good at. Something nice you have done for someone else. And get that voice in your head to say, "Well done! You did a good thing there."

CLOSING

Don't let the person who criticizes you most be YOU.

It's *your* life: it's *your* voice: so make it a *good* voice.

Notes:

Cysylltu hwn gyda adeg e ddiogelwch?

a tynnu 'selfie'?

17

BRITISH REACTION
TO THE NAZI THREAT

AIM: To teach about recent history and standing up for oneself.

In this assembly, the author has referred to his own mother as a way
of bringing immediacy to the story. You may adapt this to refer to
someone else you know who would have had similar experiences.

HOOK

What a great day! (insert today's date). A unique day. And a great
one. That's a good place to be, and a good time to be alive! We have
so much to look forward to this term, indeed, this year: (List some
upcoming events / trips / new features at the school as appropriate)

It's great isn't it? All looks good. That's where we are now; looking
forward to a new term, a new year, a new and exciting period in our
lives. But I want us today, to think a bit more carefully about exactly
how we got here. Did we do it all by ourselves?

It has been said that if you *really* want to understand the place you
live in, you should go and live somewhere very different. Then, when
you come back, you understand your own place better - by contrast.

The same is true of *where* we are now in time. Sometimes you need to look back into the past, in order to better understand and appreciate the present, and the future.

OVERVIEW

Let's go back to 1940 (as appropriate) years ago. Could things have been any more different? Hardly! There was no technology then of course. Well, there was some rudimentary technology I suppose, but nothing like we have now. No ipods, no playstations, no television even. Very few telephones, and certainly no mobile phones.

But what they did have was the radio, and I want to share with you something my mother told me about listening to the radio in 1940.

MAIN POINT ONE: HOW THE NEWS OF THE DEFEAT OF THE BRITISH EXPEDITIONARY FORCE WAS RECEIVED

In my mother's street not many families had a radio. My mother's family were lucky, one of the few. And so when something important like a big news announcement came on, my grandmother would invite the neighbours in to listen.

And sure, there were some pretty big news stories in 1940. But you already know that, don't you? Let's just remind ourselves.

In the 1930's many people were poor. My mother's family certainly was. So was everyone they knew. And it wasn't just in England. Throughout the world people were suffering poverty because of the great depression. Different countries reacted to this in different ways.

In Germany, Adolf Hitler was known as 'das Fuhrer' meaning 'the leader' or 'guide' for the nation. Hitler decided that the best way to deal with the great depression was to make war on just about everybody he didn't like - which turned out to be an awful lot of people. He set up his own political party, the Nazi party, with the ambition of taking on the world.

According to the Nazis, the basic idea was that German people were the best in the world and everyone else should be their slaves. It almost sounds like a joke; 'We will rule the world!' But, as you probably already know, it was actually very true.

So, everyone in England was nervous to say the least. We had not built up a very big army. Hitler had. We were not prepared for war. Hitler was. So whenever my grandmother heard that an important news announcement was coming, she would invite all the neighbours round to listen to the radio.

My mum remembers those occasions very clearly to this day. She told me that she didn't always fully understand what was happening – she was only about ten at the time - but she remembers those occasions when the neighbours gathered in her mother's living room, listening to the news.

One time she describes so well, was the news broadcast saying that France had just surrendered to Germany, and although she didn't really understand what was happening, she certainly remembers the reaction from the adults. Everyone around that kitchen table on that day was silent for a long while. Slowly, in ones or two's they went home. They hardly said a word. They just left.

My grandmother slumped onto a chair and put her head in her hands.

If the French had given up, what chance did we have? We knew it was our turn next. They Germans would certainly invade. They would probably win. They would kill many of us, wound many more and make us all their servants.

They would be able to attack us now, not just from Germany but also from France. They had a huge army and air force. We did not. We could, then, have slumped into defeatism. Defeatism is when you know you are going to lose even before you fight.

But we didn't. And do you know why? It's because my gran's neighbours had been invited to her house to listen to the radio on a previous important occasion. They had all been there once before - at another time when England expected the worst.

At the beginning of June they had all gone into her kitchen to listen to the Prime Minister speak.

MAIN POINT TWO: THE RALLYING CRY

Our entire army had just been rescued from France where it looked as though they were going to be smashed to pieces. We wanted to hear what the Prime Minister, Winston Churchill had to say.

What was the future? How could we cope?

Well, this is what he told them:

- *We shall defend our island home...if necessary for years; if necessary, alone.*
- *We shall go on to the end, we shall fight in France,*
- *we shall fight on the seas and oceans,*
- *we shall fight with growing confidence and growing strength in the air,*
- *we shall defend our Island, whatever the cost may be,*
- *we shall fight on the beaches,*
- *we shall fight on the landing grounds,*
- *we shall fight in the fields and in the streets,*
- *we shall fight in the hills;*
- *we shall never surrender.*

And of course, we did not surrender after this famous speech because the British people had been given *new* hope. More than hope, they were given courage and unshakeable belief. No matter how bad things got in those dark days we would *not* give up, *ever*!

Now, my mother has told me stories about her childhood more times than I can remember. But I never tire of hearing them. When I was a little boy I enjoyed hearing them because of the excitement of hearing about the Second World War. Like the time when my mum saw a German fighter plane shot down. It crashed in a field behind her house. That was real drama.

But now that I am older I think less about the drama and more about the tragedy. The poor man who my mum saw burn to death in the wreckage of his plane. He had family too, and a mother of his own who would never see him again.

MAIN POINT THREE: THE BATTLE OF BRITAIN

1940 was the year of The Battle of Britain. Hitler was ready to invade England. He had the soldiers and he had the tanks, and he had a lot more planes than we had. But surprisingly, what he *didn't* have was control of the air and that was going to prove crucial in the battle for Britain.

Because, in a small factory in Birmingham we were making a new kind of plane. It was called the Spitfire. But we didn't really have enough of them - surely not enough to fight off the entire, massive German air force, the Luftwaffe. There were so few pilots that sometimes every single one of them was in the air at the same time.

But eventually the Germans gave up. They knew if they couldn't beat the air force, they couldn't invade.

The English people were so relieved. Germany and the Nazis could not invade. They could not beat us.

Winston Churchill, who was very good with words said, "Never has so much been owed by so many, to so few."

SUMMARY

Looking back it is easy to see how the whole country could have given up then. It looked as though it was all over. But as Churchill said, "when you're going through Hell, keep going!" So we didn't give up. And that's the main reason why we're still free today, and looking towards a brighter future.

CLOSING

And so, as we look at the world in <u>(current year)</u> we see a very different place. We live a life of relative luxury. We live a life of convenience and peace, free from the danger of invasion by an enemy. So if we really want to appreciate the good things we have - especially our freedom and our hopes for a better future - it's sometimes best to look at the past - in contrast - and be grateful to those who just wouldn't give up! History has *a lot* to teach us.

I will finish on a lighter note: Winston Churchill was a surprising man for a number of reasons. He was good with words of course, but he also lived to the ripe old age of 90. This is all the more surprising because he smoked cigars constantly. He also drank a lot.

Once, it was quite late in the evening and he had been drinking rather heavily. As he walked, or rather, staggered along the corridors of the Houses of Parliament, he bumped into a lady M.P. She stared at him angrily and said,

"Sir, you are drunk!"

To which he replied:

"Madam, you are ugly. But in the morning, I shall be sober!"

18

SMOKING

AIM:To reinforce anti-smoking measures

HOOK

Some people say that teachers shouldn't make judgements; that we shouldn't try to tell you what's right and what's wrong. These people say that we should just inform you of *the facts* and let you make your own judgements and decisions.

Well, I don't completely agree with those people. I think that one of the main responsibilities of a teacher is to bring attention to important issues, and to encourage students to make *wise* decisions. And you cannot make wise decisions if you don't know all the facts - right?

Well, we already know that taking *illegal* drugs is not only a crime, but that there are serious health risks and many negative social consequences. So clearly, taking illegal drugs is *not* a wise decision.

But you know what? There is another drug - quite legal - and it's the biggest heart-breaker, the biggest killer of them all.

Can anyone tell me what it is?

OVERVIEW

That's right; tobacco! And because it is *legal* and widely used, this makes it all the more dangerous. You may think it isn't necessary to talk to you about the dangers of smoking. You may think you already know it all. Well, you don't. Because no one knows; *no one*. Not even the best, most qualified doctors really know all of the dangers you are exposing yourself to. So we will be looking this morning at the horrors and dangers of smoking and at how you can avoid them.

MAIN POINT ONE: HEALTH

Thousands of people die every year as a result of smoking cigarettes. The combined effects of nicotine (the main drug in tobacco) and other gases which enter the lungs when smoking, greatly increase the chance of disease and ill-health.

Smoking has been directly linked to lung cancer, heart disease and other major illnesses, as well as being dangerous during pregnancy for the mother *and* the unborn child.

Secondary smoking or passive smoking can also put the health of others at risk. This is one of the reasons why smoking has been so widely banned in public places.

MAIN POINT TWO: ACTION BEING TAKEN BY GOVERNMENTS

Governments in Europe, America and other advanced countries are taking action to make it harder for people to start smoking. Ever since 2006 it has been against the law to smoke indoors in a public place. Health warnings are also on cigarette packets and cartons, and other, new laws are on the way.

And why? To save your lives, of course. Some of the health warnings on cigarette packets can be quite shocking. They show pictures of diseased bodies; diseased - it's not a nice word. Dis-eased.

MAIN POINT THREE: SO MANY PEOPLE DO IT – BUT YOU CAN AVOID IT

Why do we continue to do it? We all know it's dumb. Worse than dumb - it's *deadly*. So why do it?

You know, back in my parents' day they didn't know smoking was bad for you. They guessed that *maybe* it might not be good for you but they actually didn't know for sure. But by the time I was your age, we all knew. Yet still, people smoked.

Now, (<u>todays date</u>) we know even more about how bad smoking is. Yet *still* people start smoking. Although the number of adults who smoke has dropped over the past ten years, this has not happened amongst young people. In fact in some parts of the country the number of young smokers has actually *increased*, especially amongst young women.

Statistics have shown that one quarter of Britain's 15-year-olds (both boys and girls) are regular smokers. It is estimated that 450 children per day *start* smoking. Half of all teenagers who are currently smoking will die from diseases caused by tobacco if they continue to smoke throughout their lives, and one half of this number will have their lives shortened by an average of 23 years.

Currently one in five 15-year-old boys smokes cigarettes - this is a decrease of 5% since the mid 1980's. But the numbers of teenage girls smoking has risen from 25% in the mid 1980s to 29% now - that's one in three - a disturbing increase.

So why do young people start smoking? Well, apparently because 'it looks cool'. That's how it usually starts anyway. You see someone you admire smoking, and they look so 'cool', so you try it too. But there's nothing 'cool' about losing 23 years of your life. There's nothing 'cool' about being sick and unhealthy; and there's nothing 'cool' about throwing good money away - is there?

Young people think, *"I'll just try it once - just to be cool - just to fit in with my friends."* But they're forgetting something *very* important. Cigarretes contain nicotene, and nicotene is an *addictive* drug, just like all the illegal drugs like heroin and cocaine. The nicotene is in there for a reason - it's to make you continue smoking long after you realise it's not 'cool' any more. This is how the tobacco companies make so much money. A little chemical change takes place in the smoker's head which says, *"You must carry on! You have to have another smoke!"* And we all know how powerful that little voice in our heads can be. But we also know that *you* can control what you think.

So if ever you feel really tempted, remember this. *You* are stronger, *you* can tell smoking to get lost! 450 new smokers every day? Does this sound like a wise choice? Then don't let one of them be you.

SUMMARY

We have seen that smoking is a very dangerous habit indeed; we have seen that many people begin smoking even though they know the risks; that governments across the world are trying to save their own people from falling victims; and that the big tobacco companies are only interested in our money. We know that in the fight against the awful diseases this habit can cause, our greatest weapon is our own personal determination to say 'No!'

CLOSING

So for all those of you who have not started smoking - (and I know that's nearly all of you). - please don't start. And for those of you who *have* started. Please stop! Stop now, or get help. You *can* beat it. You are the boss. Don't let that annoying little voice in your head take over. Don't let the tobacco companies control you. Don't let them take away your health, your money, your life.

Show them who's really the boss. *You* are!

19

TECHNOLOGY

*AIM:To encourage children to take a greater interest in the
fantastic contribution technology is making to our lives*

HOOK

- Is there anyone in the room who has seen a Harry Potter film?
- What about Dr.Who, Star Trek, James Bond. Ever seen those?

The famous inventor James Dyson recently wrote an article stating
that children should not be so obsessed with Harry Potter and
science-fiction fantasy. He felt that children were being distracted
by this fantasy genre and therefore knew nothing about *real* science.

'Real science', he felt, was much more exciting and useful than
things like the *Twilight* series or other science-fiction fantasies.

OVERVIEW

But when we look at all the evidence, I am not so sure that I agree
with him. Because that which was considered to be science *fiction*
only thirty years ago is becoming science *fact* now.

Today, we are going to look at a surprisingly large number of
so-called 'science-fiction' ideas, which have since turned into reality.

MAIN POINT ONE: EXAMPLES OF SCIENCE FICTION THAT HAVE BECOME REALITY

For example; in one scene from the Harry Potter series, Harry says a magic word and a mysterious door opens in front of him.

This sort of 'magic' is actually very easy to do - scientifically that is - because computers now have voice recognition. You can now program a computer to operate an electric motor that opens a door in response to the words 'open sesame' and so create a magical portal.

Have any of you seen James Bond in the film *Gold Finger*? He had a device on his car that could track the baddie on a map, showing him where he had gone, so he could follow at a distance. I remember thinking, "Wow, wouldn't it be great to have one of those." However in 1965 this was pure science fiction. But today we use satellite navigation all the time, and tracking programs for mobile phones are just as common.

Star Trek in the late 1960's predicted computers that would be able to talk to you - a crazy notion at the time. But this has certainly happened now: You can talk to a computer and it will do what you ask, or, if you've got poor eyesight, computers can read the text audibly to you at the click of a mouse.

Or Captain Kirk's communicator; just a small box that flipped open so he could have a chat with Spock. Well, today's mobile phones do exactly this - don't they? I think that many modern phones are probably based on a *Star Trek* communicator or a tricorder.

Tricorders in the *Star Trek* series were used to find out where you were and what was around you. 'What a fantastical idea?' we thought at the time. But today, Google maps can be downloaded onto a mobile phone and a tracking program will show where you are and give you directions to anywhere you like. It can tell you what height you are at, and even show you a satellite picture of where you are standing. As you move, the dot representing you moves with you.

Science *fiction* only thirty years ago - science *fact* today!

In fact some modern phones do far more than the science fiction devices they seem to have been based upon. In *The Lord of the Rings* by J R Tolkien for example, the mysterious *Palantir of Orthanc* enables you to see things that are happening far away or even to see people in far-away places and talk to them. Today's *Skype* is good for video communications and nearly every town has a web cam that you can log onto to see what is going on.

MAIN POINT TWO: THEY DIDN'T ALWAYS GET IT RIGHT – WE NEED ACTUAL SCIENCE

However, not all science fiction series got it right. One series called *Space 1999* showed a member of the moon-base making a calculation on a slide rule. If any of you here know what a slide rule is I will be astonished. It was a hand-held device used for doing complex calculations before the invention of the electronic calculator. Today, it is all-but obsolete.

I wonder if the people who design and build modern marvels like computers and the internet, ever read or watched science fiction fantasy in the 1960's ? I'll bet you they did! Bill Gates, the founder of Microsoft, is a huge science fiction fan. He loves *Star Trek* and *Star Wars* and today he is one of the richest men in the world.

However, in some ways I do agree with Mr Dyson, and his concerns that not enough people study 'real' science. It's fine just reading science fiction and fantasy and the fabulous ideas they have, but without scientists and engineers to make these fantasies into reality there would be no mobile phones, computer games or the internet.

So it's clear that we need both: People with fantastic imaginations, as well as scientists and engineers. And I wonder what particular things and mad fiction ideas that we are reading about today, will become scientific fact in 30 years' time?

A broom that flies perhaps? Planes that go up into space and defy gravity are already being developed. In one of these you would be able to go to Australia for lunch and be back home in time for tea. Will someone develop a time machine like Dr Who's tardis? Will we be able to teleport instantly anywhere?

It's so hard to guess what will become reality in the future and people have often got it so wrong, as we see in the following topical quotes:

> In 1957 the Astronomer Royal of Britain stated that 'space travel is bunk'. He was slightly embarrassed two weeks later when the Russian space ship Sputnik went into orbit.

> "I think there is a world market for maybe five computers" said Thomas Watson chairman of IBM 1943.

> "Heavier than air flying machines are impossible" said Lord Kelvin, President of the Royal Society in 1895.

> "This telephone has too many shortcomings to be seriously considered as a means of communication. The device is inherently of no value to us," – that was a Western Union internal memo (now the largest telephone company in America).

SUMMARY

So, what does the future hold? We can't accurately predict all the possibilities, but many creative artists have imagined what *could* possibly happen, only for us to find, sometimes just a short time afterwards, that what they imagined has actually come true.

CLOSING

So the next time someone says to you 'that is impossible' don't believe them. Trust your imagination, and one day, with a little bit of help from science and technology, *anything* may be possible.

20

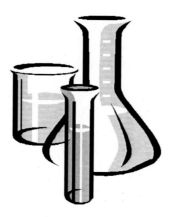

THE MIRACLE OF SCIENCE

AIM: To raise awareness of the impact of science on our lives

HOOK

Read out the following names to the assembly, and ask the pupils to vote on whether they think the person is a famous scientist.

Select at random a pupil who has voted and ask them if they know what that scientist did, and why their discovery was useful. Ask the pupil to share their answer with the rest of the assembly if applicable.

Albert Einstein – (Scientist) Proposed the theory of relativity.

Sir Isaac Newton – (Scientist) Most famous for explaining the laws of motion.

Katie Price – (TV celebrity) Famous for being famous

Charles Darwin – (Scientist) Proposed the theory of evolution

Usain Bolt- Famous athlete sprinter

Michael Faraday – (Scientist) The 'father' of electricity

Wayne Rooney – Famous footballer

James Cook – Famous explorer

Alexander Graham Bell – (Scientist) Invented the telephone and the metal detector

Christopher Columbus – Famous explorer

Thomas Alva Edison – (Scientist) Invented the light bulb and the phonograph, amongst other inventions

When most of you think about science, you might picture yourself in a boring chemistry lesson learning about the importance of a catalyst, and think; "When am I ever going to need to need to know *this* in my life," and in some cases I agree. Some formulas and experiments are really only for the specialists. But before you totally switch off from science lessons, just take a moment to think about all of the things you use in your day-to-day life, for which we owe science and scientists the real credit.

<u>Allow the assembly 30 seconds to think.</u>

How many of you use a Playstation X-box or Wii; how many of you turn on a light bulb and don't think anything of it; how many of you use a computer and go on to the internet daily? All of these and much, much more of what you use and take for granted every day, would never have been invented or created if we did not have science or the scientific method.

Some of you are probably thinking WHY? How is a Playstation, Wii or a Light bulb in anyway 'scientific?' Well, the truth of the matter is that it has taken over 200 years of scientific discovery and understanding to get to the point where we can create a console like the Wii or Playstation. Aspects such as the laser that reads the CD, the transistors, resistors, infra red and electricity all took time to reach the level where they could be used to power things like your games console, light bulbs and personal computers.

OVERVIEW

Science, therefore and the scientific method of proving or disproving a theory, has allowed us to create truly amazing things, that have made our own lives easier and far more enjoyable. Let's explore this today. Let's find out where science has really brought us.

MAIN POINT ONE: MEDICAL BENEFITS

Although various scientific discoveries have made our lives easier and more enjoyable, many scientific discoveries in the fields of chemistry and biology have also saved numerous lives. The filtering and purification of water for example, now means that diseases such as polio, typhoid and cholera that come from drinking polluted water, are now - at least in this country - a thing of the past. The invention of antibiotics has also saved numerous lives, and is still used today to fight off many common infections which, if left untreated, could be potentially fatal.

Scientists are still working today on some of the biggest problems that exist: the cure for cancer; alternative energy sources; and explaining why we are here in the first place, to name but a few.

Although science does not have *all* the answers, and you may reasonably question some of its findings; just look back in history at the scientific discoveries that were made in the last 200 years and how far mankind has come, and you'll see that science is invaluable.

MAIN POINT TWO: BENEFITS BROUGHT TO THE WORLD OF LEISURE

The next time you are in a science lesson thinking; "Why am I learning about a catalyst and what use will it be to me in *my* life?" Just think about your Wii, Computer and Playstation, and how, without determined scientists you would not have any of them. Neither would you have *You Tube*, iphones, or your favourite consoles and video games that you go home to every day after school - and no doubt take for granted - right?

MAIN POINT THREE: WHERE WOULD WE BE WITHOUT SCIENCE?

If there had never been science lessons, there would have been no scientists; if there had been no scientists, there would have been no great inventions; and with no great inventions there would be no telephones, no cars, no trains, no planes. Then where would we be?

SUMMARY

We have seen today that many of the *greatest* people in the world are not necessarily *famous* people. And that many *famous* people today are not really all that *great* - right? But if we were to give proper credit to all those determined scientists who have made our modern life so much better by their efforts and inventions, I think we could all agree that science, the scientific method, and scientists in general, are really 'great'.

CLOSING

So do pay attention in your next science lesson. After all, you may be destined for greatness. Who knows what *you* might invent?

LIFE DECISIONS

AIM: To encourage young people to consider their future

<u>HOOK</u>

Which way?

Which is the best / quickest / easiest way to.......... <u>(mention an area of the school or local community which may be approached from a variety of different routes.)?</u>

We all ask this type of simple question from time to time. To ask directions; to make decisions; to ask for help or guidance.

Some questions have simple answers, for instance:

- Which is the way to the station?

- Which way shall we go for our run?

But other questions require more thought. For example:

- Which way shall we go to London?

The answer could be by plane, train, car, coach, bus, bike or walk, depending on where you are starting from. Your choice will also depend on the reason for your journey. Is it urgent? Is it for pleasure? Is it for business? What will it cost me? How much luggage must I bring? How will I plan for it - or should I just leave it all to luck?

And what about *life's* decisions? For isn't life just a great journey too? In many ways, life is a one-way journey that requires careful planning and wise choices. We can't just go back and buy another ticket and start all over again. The decisions we make will determine *where* we end up, and *what sort* of a journey we have through life.

The big question is; will it be a happy journey? An interesting and productive journey? Or will it be something else?

So much depends on the life-decisions we make.

OVERVIEW

During life we all have to make decisions that affect our immediate comfort, our mood, or even our futures. Sometimes, decisions are made *for* us, and we are obliged to go a certain way, but most of the time, the *really* important decisions are left up to us: Do I apply myself at school, for example. Or, who will I chose as friends? Or, how do I develop and maintain a good character?

It's very exciting to be your age in so many ways, because your life-journey is only at the beginning. And the routes you take will largely be down to your own personal decisions. But will you make good decisions, poor decisions - or just leave it all to luck? Because if you don't make good life-decisions when you have the chance, then often, other people will make those decisions *for* you, and you may not always like those choices. Let's explore this a bit further.

MAIN POINT ONE – A LUCKY STORY

I remember a story about a young man who was illiterate - who couldn't read or write - because he hadn't applied himself properly at school. But this is the story of a very *lucky* young man, because he was soon able to get a job as a gardener, because *luckily*, his uncle found him a job. He took his instructions directly from the head gardener each day, and he did his best at work. But when a new employer realised he was illiterate, he sacked the young man because he felt he wouldn't be able to do a good job if he couldn't read the new employer's instructions. And of course, he was right.

Dejected, the young man realised that without his job he couldn't pay his rent, and he prepared himself for the worst. But on his way home he noticed an advertisement in a barber's shop for a general handyman. *Luckily* there was no application form to fill out, and the barber needed someone right away, so the young man got the job. 'This must be fate!' he thought. He knew he was *very* lucky indeed. He would still have an income. He was so willing and conscientious that his employer trained him to cut hair and help out at busy times. He was good at cutting hair and many customers asked for him. And *luckily* for him, he didn't need to follow any written instructions.

Eventually, after many years the (now not-so-young) man had saved enough money to open his own shop. 'What a lucky guy,' everyone thought, and everyone expected him to do very well. But because he was illiterate, and because he was too embarrassed to tell his customers about it, the man had to secretly employ other people to fill out all the necessary forms, keep the accounts and deal with the tax people.. which ended up costing him a lot of money and gave him lot's and lot's of stress. Eventually, all the money he'd saved up was gone. Now, he wasn't feeling quite so lucky after all, and really, *really* wished that he'd applied himself better at school.

Broke and homeless, he now realised that he should have made better life-decisions when he had the opportunity. That he shouldn't have relied on luck, fate and other people's decisions to shape his life. He had been so very lucky after all. Just imagine what he could have achieved by making the right life-decisions when he had the chance.

Lucky? Really? What do *you* think?

MAIN POINT TWO – TAKE RESPONSIBILITY FOR YOUR DECISIONS

It's no good relying on luck or fate or the generosity of others when it comes to the major decisions in life. Sure, some of us may get an occasional lucky break, but that's no way to plan the most important journey of all - is it? Would anyone here set out on an important journey without first checking that we're heading in the right direction? That we have sufficient food for the journey? That there's some realistic chance of us getting where we're going to? Of course not. So how many of you really know what you want to do in life? (Ask for a show of hands perhaps?)

Whatever the case, we all need to do some planning, and the sooner the planning is started, the more likely you are to have control over the way you want to go, and how you get there. You have many working years ahead of you - if you are lucky - and you need to make them as interesting and rewarding as you can. Now is the time to think ahead. What do we need to do *now* to achieve our goals?

SUMMARY

We began by considering the best way to get to (the place mentioned at the beginning), and we saw that there are many different routes. Relying on fate, luck and the generosity of others is one choice, but clearly not the best one. We need to start planning now.

CLOSING

Ways to go:

- Working for yourself – what do you need?
- Training for a trade or profession – what do you need?
- Training for an athletic career – what do you need?
- Training for a caring profession such as nursing, teaching, social care, or care worker - what do you need?

The decision, ladies and gentlemen, is yours!

22

WORDS OF WISDOM

AIM: To show the value of thinking before you speak

HOOK

One evening a man came home from work. He had had a busy, unpleasant day and snapped at his teenage son as soon as he came in. His son, who *had* been pleased to see him, rushed out of the house upset and bumped into a girl, telling her angrily to, "look where you're going!"

This upset the girl of course, who went home and was rude to her mother when her mother asked if she'd had a good day? Her mother was hurt by her daughter's rudeness, and when her husband came home she complained to him about 'not being appreciated' for looking after the family.

So the husband had a row with his wife and didn't sleep well. The next morning he went to the office in a bad mood and was rude and irritable with his assistant; the father of the teenage boy.

OVERVIEW

If you've followed this story you'll see that your unkind acts can often affect others, and that the whole circle can come back to upset you. Sometimes when we feel bad, we take it out on others. You don't need me to tell you that this is unfair. And, as we have just seen it can lead to some pretty serious consequences. Today we are going to consider one way you can take control of your life.

MAIN POINT – HOW YOU CAN TAKE CONTROL

How can you help yourself become a happier and more successful person? ...Interested?

First of all, try to believe in yourself and never think of yourself as a failure, because you never really *fail* provided you sincerely *try*. You just have a setback, which is normal part of life. We can all overcome setbacks.

When you learn to walk for instance, you topple over many times before you succeed, but everyone who is physically able to, learns to walk. In the same way you can learn how to value yourself.

But it's not always going to be easy.

You may say to me, 'But I *do* value myself. I know how good I am and that my opinions are right, and I don't really care what other people think!'

But does this attitude really make you *happy*? Is it really the best way to view the world? Is it appropriate that we *only* consider our *own* opinions and points of view - without any regard for others?

If you do not open yourself to different points of view, or if you think you always know best, you miss chances for learning as well as opportunities for understanding and helping others.

Here are a few tips:

1. Think before you speak.

2. Take an active interest in your lessons and you may be surprised at how interesting they become.

3. Do not listen to gossip, or if you hear gossip, don't repeat it.

4. Be polite and pleasant: this will get you what you want more often than rudeness.

SUMMARY

We have seen just how easy it is to take offence and fly off the handle; we've also seen how, if we take a moment to think of all the possible repercussions, we can calm down and make better choices.

We know that we can all be a lot happier if we just take a moment to reflect.

CLOSING

Let's do that now. When was the last time you felt really angry? Would things have gone better if you had taken longer to think about the best thing to do? I expect so. So let's all try to be a bit more understanding, and a bit kinder to each other.

Thank you for listening, and have a good day!

Notes:

23

EDUCATION: "YOU DON'T KNOW HOW LUCKY YOU ARE"

AIM: To foster an appreciation of education and an awareness of its historical development.

HOOK

Questions (Hands Up)

How many of you were looking forward to coming into school today?

How many of you don't mid coming into school today?

How many of you were not looking forward to coming into school today?

Well, here we are in school anyway, and hopefully it will be a rewarding day for us all. And although I am sure most of you are thinking of hundreds of other things you would prefer to be doing right now, the majority of you probably don't realise how very lucky you are to live in a time where education is provided to everyone, no matter what their background, race or colour. This is a wonderful thing. It may not always feel like it, but it really and truly is.

OVERVIEW

Let me explain: Education has always been considered 'a privilege' - something we should all be very grateful for. But education has not always been free like we have it today. So today we're going to find out how the wonderful circumstances *we* enjoy all came about.

MAIN POINT ONE - FREE EDUCATION

There was a time many years ago when education was only accessible to the extremely wealthy, or extremely intelligent, and sometimes even the extremely intelligent were denied education if they or their parents did not have the money to afford it.

Sunday schools were started in the 18th century to teach boys to read the bible and learn catechism, and in the 19th century the state became involved in funding schools. But it wasn't until 1880 that education became compulsory between the ages of 5 and 10. In 1900 higher elementary education covered the ages of 10 to 15.

The 1944 Education Act that made education compulsory was the start of the modern system of education. That's only (70) years ago!

So it has only been in the last 70 years that education, specifically secondary education, has been compulsory and available to all; no matter what your economic background or intelligence. Although to you 70 years might seem a long time ago, just take a moment to think how old your grandmother or great grandmother is, and compare that to the 70 years that secondary education has been available for. It really isn't that long ago - is it?

Thankfully, today in the UK things are different, and everyone is given education and a fair chance to become, or progress to, whatever they choose, depending on the effort they put in; something that could quite probably have been denied to your grandmother or great grandmother 70 years ago.

Now although a lot of you *do* appreciate this opportunity and *do* try hard in school, there are those who would rather, if they had the choice, not attend school. They would rather pack it all in and go home and watch Jeremy Kyle. Unfortunately what those people do not realise is that they will need something in the future that they won't be able to get without a good education and qualifications. That 'something' is necessary for you to survive in the modern world. Can anyone guess what it is?'

A job!

MAIN POINT TWO: THE NEED FOR QUALIFICATIONS

Now I am not denying there was a time many years ago when it was relatively easy to get a job without any, or very few qualifications, partly owing to the fact that very few people got into secondary school, because at the time England still had large numbers of manufacturing industries. But now, for better or for worse, this is no longer the case, and most employers do not just *expect* qualifications for the majority of jobs, they *demand* them!

For example; an average worker working for about £16,000 a year is expected to have some form of qualification for the jobs available at that payment level. When you think about the rent, bills, food and other expenditure you will have to pay as an adult, that really doesn't work out to very much left to spend on yourself, or on other personal things like a car, a mobile phone, socialising etc.

School therefore is important if you want a lifestyle where you can afford some of the finer things in life, such as having a nice house, owning a car, eating well and healthy, going on holidays and generally enjoying yourself. It is no longer the case in society where you can come out of school with very few qualifications and still expect to get a job with no problems, especially with the competition that now exists for jobs in the working world, and the expectation of good qualifications from the majority of employers.

SUMMARY

So the next time any of you think to yourself; *'I would rather be at home watching TV than be here at school learning how to create a website..'* Just remember:

- At least you have been given the opportunity to attend school, no matter what your economic background, colour, class, or intellectual abilities.
- That you have been given a fair chance to get the qualifications needed to gain a good job.
- That you also have the opportunity to progress to further education such as college or university - and from there, who knows where?

For the majority of working-class people 70 years ago, hardly any of this was possible, and young people such as yourselves had little choice but to resign themselves to a life of hard labour or servitude - very poorly paid - with little or no prospects to better themselves.

Today, courses are provided by Higher Education Colleges to help those who struggled at school, to help them obtain the qualifications they need to improve their employment prospects. But going back to college as an independent adult - with all the costs and responsibilities that entails - is never going to be as easy as learning at school. So make sure you make the most of it while you can.

CLOSING

Today we have free access to education for all, and I hope you are now beginning to appreciate what a truly wonderful thing education is? Is there anyone here who would rather go back to the 1940's?

Let's hope then, that you're also beginning to realise, how lucky you really are?

24

TRY ANYTHING ONCE

AIM: To encourage young people to try new hobbies and interests, this assembly makes the point through a dramatic and amusing story

HOOK

I know that it may not always seem like it, but I love my job. Some students came to see me yesterday to ask if we could set up a new (as appropriate) club. I have to tell you, it was a real treat to me to talk with those students about how and when it could be done. And next term, we will look at setting up a (as appropriate) club. I hope a lot of you will think about joining.

It's always a pleasure to see young people like you develop, and take on new interests and hobbies, some of which will bring pleasure to you for your whole lives. If I can help even in a small way, that's great. And that's why I love this job. There's something new happening every day. New challenges, and new opportunities.

OVERVIEW

But you know, I didn't always want to be a teacher. When I started out in the workforce I was unsure. I thought first about becoming a journalist. I wanted to write the stories they use in newspapers and magazines. I thought that maybe I would be able to tell a good story. I managed while still at school, to get some work experience with my local paper. You know, older students at our school also do work experience, and most of them I know, have a great time. I'd like to tell you what happened when I looked for my first story to write. What happened is almost unbelievable.

MAIN POINT: THE STORY

My work experience was with the local paper. To be honest, for the first three days they gave me really boring jobs like tidying the office or making tea for the editor. But then on the third day, they sent me out to get a story of my own. They said;

> *"Look, there's a travelling circus just come to town. Why don't you ring them up and ask them if they could give us an interesting story. There must be <u>something</u> interesting happening in a circus."*

So that's what I did, and I was told the most amazing story I have ever heard in my life. I want to share it with you today.

I didn't phone up the circus. I went straight there on my bike to meet the owner of the circus. I just went straight to his office – which was in a caravan – and knocked on the door. I didn't tell him I was still at school. I said I had come from the paper and that we would like to write about his circus. He said;

> *"I'll tell you what I'll do. I give you a story if you let me have a whole page, free advert in your newspaper."*

Well I knew that a small advert in the paper cost a lot of money - but a whole page! But I wanted a story. So I said, 'Yes, no problem.'

This is what he told me. I think you're going to like it. It certainly makes a point.

The circus, he said, was doing well now. But it hadn't always been the case. At one time they were going broke. No one was coming to watch their show, or at least, very few. And the owner was desperate. He thought it was because the acts they had were maybe too boring. So he advertised for new performers.

NEW EXCITING ACTS NEEDED FOR CIRCUS
HIGH RATES OF PAY FOR REALLY GOOD PERFORMERS

But no one replied.

Then, one day, a small, chubby, rather ordinary-looking man walked shyly into the owner's office.

> "I've come about the advert. Circus performer."
> "Oh, what do you do?"
> "I will do two things. I will persuade a lion to open its mouth and I will put my head inside. When my head is well inside the lion's mouth I will sing God Save the Queen before removing my head. Then, I will climb one hundred feet up a ladder to the roof of The Big Top and I will dive off into a tank of water placed on the floor containing only one metre of water."

Well, the owner was stunned. An act like this would surely bring in the customers.

> "OK, but first show me. I'll have the boys bring the lion cage into the Big Top and have a tank of water put under the ladder."

Word got round the circus of what was about to happen and every one who worked there gathered round to watch this amazing act. They wondered about a man who would take such enormous risks.

First the shy little man approached a lion in its cage. He stared into its eyes and then held its head. Very gently he prized the lions mouth open. When the mouth was really wide, he put his head inside. He sang God Save the Queen. He sang badly. But that was hardly the point.

He took his head out. He climbed the ladder. One hundred feet off the ground. he launched himself into the air. He was rather fat and flabby; his skin wobbled as he hurtled downwards. He hit the water with a tremendous crash.

It all went deathly quiet. Then, after a moment, his chubby face appeared over the side of the tank. He was unhurt. The circus workers cheered wildly.

The owner went over to him and said,
"That was fantastic. You've got the job."
But the short, fat, bald, shy man shook his head.
"No, don't want it."
"But that was the most amazing thing I've ever seen. Look, I'll pay you £100 a week."

That was a lot of money then, but the man still shook his head.
"No."
"Alright. £150."
"No."
"It was so good. Look £200 a week. I can't pay more."
"NO."
"Ok, I give up. But tell me, why won't you take the job? You were absolutely brilliant!"
The short, fat, bald, shy man thought for a moment, cleared his throat and said, "I've never done anything like that before. Didn't like it."

And he was never seen again.

SUMMARY

Now here's the point. Most of you enjoy your own favourite sports or activities, don't you? You boys enjoy .... And the girls enjoy.................. (mention some popular sports or activities here). You do these things many times day after day, and why not.?You enjoy these things, you like doing them and you're probably getting very good too.

But why not try something new?

At school, we offer so many opportunities to try something new.

We are not asking you to stick your head in a lion's mouth. We won't ask you to throw yourself into a tank of water. We don't ask you to really risk anything. - just a bit of your time.

At this school we offer you walking in the mountains, canoeing, drama, choirs.... (add your own school's activities here). Don't be a stick-in-the-mud. Make a decision. This term, try something new.

You might be surprised. You might like it. You might be very good at it. It might even change your life.

CLOSING

And the circus?

Well, that was a tall story in more ways than one. It may even have been made up! Actually if someone really dived into a pool like that without years and years of training, they would probably be badly injured or even killed. And putting your head in a lion's mouth would be ridiculously dangerous - especially if he's hungry! Don't do it at home folks. It was only a story. But heck, it's a good story and if it makes you think about starting a new hobby, I'd say it was worth it.

Notes:

25

NELSON MANDELA

*AIM: To raise awareness of recent history
and the value of reconciliation*

HOOK

Throughout the history of this world, there have been times when the strong have ganged up and made life miserable for the weak. They have used their power to make life miserable for those weaker than themselves. It's sad, but true.

But it's also true that throughout the history of this world, some brave people have stood up to the bullies and said;

"This is not fair, this has to change."

Sometimes these brave people have done so at great risk to themselves. Often, they have paid a high personal price.

OVERVIEW

It's about such a person that I want to talk today. You will surely have heard of Nelson Mandela. He fought for what he knew was right. Listen to his story. Could *you* be this brave and forgiving?

MAIN POINT ONE: EARLY LIFE

Nelson Mandela was born in South Africa in 1918. He was the first member of his family to go to school. He always thought it was vital to get educated. He worked very hard at school. So much so that he became a lawyer. His job, the one that he wanted, was to help poor black people when they got into difficulties with the law.

It was a job that he loved, and he was so glad that he had been educated well enough to do such a useful thing.

But something happened in his country. Something that made him feel he had an even more important role in life. He had to fight apartheid.

Taking on apartheid was an epic fight that lasted most of his life. A fight that nearly killed him.

MAIN POINT TWO: APARTHEID

What exactly was apartheid?

Basically, 'apartheid' was the name given to a whole lot of laws that forced black and white people to live completely separate lives. These laws came into force in 1948, when Nelson was 30. The government - the people who made the laws - were all white people. Even though black people outnumbered the white people in South Africa by a huge amount the white ruling class wouldn't allow black people to be in the government. The apartheid laws basically meant that black and white people had to live apart.

They had to live in different towns, for example. Black people couldn't set up a business in a white area. They couldn't enjoy the same leisure facilities – there were white beaches and black beaches and if you went to the wrong one, you could go to jail.

There were black buses and white buses with separate bus stops. Black and white men and women could not have relationships with each other. If a black man went out with a white woman or the other way about – they would be arrested.

If black people wanted to go into a white area for work, which they were sometimes allowed to do, they had to have a special pass and carry it with them all the time. Even then it could only be used in one area. If you tried to go somewhere else you would be put on trial.

All of the money in the country was with the white people. And because black people could not do business with them, it meant that black people were poor and were going to stay that way.

MAIN POINT THREE: THE STRUGGLE

So yes, it was apartheid that Nelson Mandela had to fight. He knew this system was was wrong and he was determined to fight it even if it killed him.

He wasn't the only one of course, in fact there was a group called the ANC – the African National Congress – who had decided to fight apartheid together.

Nelson soon became the most influential man in the ANC.

He had said he would give his life to the cause. But he did not want blood to be shed, and that is a most important characteristic of the man. He wanted the ANC to cause lots of problems for the white government but *not* to actually physically hurt anyone.

As time went by, Nelson Mandela could see that things might never change unless there was at least the threat of violence and so it was planned to set off a series of sabotage attacks on government-owned facilities, but always with the intention of avoiding hurting anyone.

Well, the government caught him. They put him on trial. During that trial he said;

> *"During my lifetime I have dedicated myself to the struggle of the African people. I have fought against white domination, and I have fought against black domination. I have cherished the ideal of a democratic and free society in which all persons live together in harmony and with equal opportunities. It is an ideal which I hope to live for and to achieve. But if needs be, it is an ideal for which I am prepared to die."*

Well of course, he was found guilty of planning sabotage. He spent 28 years in jail. 28 years!

In South African jails, back then, they liked very much to classify people – to put them into groups and treat them differently according to which group they were in. Nelson was in the lowest class of prisoner – a black political prisoner – which meant that his treatment was worse that any other category. For example, for many years he was allowed only one visitor and one letter every six months.

Now the main thing is that no-one ever gave up hope. The ANC did not despair, the world outside South Africa did not despair and most importantly, Nelson Mandela did not despair.

There were protests and campaigns throughout the world demanding that he should be freed and that the country should treat all of its citizens equally. There was tremendous international pressure on South Africa.

Eventually – after 28 years – the South African government agreed. They would release the man and they would start to talk about *maybe* ending apartheid. A couple of years later in 1992, that's eventually what happened.

Now the remarkable thing about Nelson Mandela is his lack of bitterness, his lack of anger. He knew that he had lost much of his life in prison because he had to fight a great injustice. But he showed no anger whatsoever against white people in general. After all, if he treated them as if they were all the same he would be no better than those who thought apartheid was a good idea.

No, what he wanted was reconciliation. Reconciliation. This means learning to accept the past and put it behind us; it means learning to agree to try to get on in the future.

South Africa's first free elections in which anyone could vote were held on 27 April 1994. The ANC won, and Mandela, as leader of the ANC became South Africa's first black President.

He was true to his word. There was no government anger against white people. This was a government of reconciliation.

This reconciliation was demonstrated beautifully in the 1995 Rugby World Cup. Black South Africans hated the South African rugby team before then. They were called the Springboks, they were always all white and they seemed to symbolize white domination over blacks. Nelson said to his people, let's support them, we are all one country now.

South Africa won the world cup, by beating New Zealand in a great game. The trophy was presented by President Nelson Mandela to the captain Francois Pienaar, who was a white Afrikaner – the very group many people thought were the most racist. Mandela was wearing a Springbok shirt with Pienaar's own number 6 on the back.

What a great symbolic moment!

SUMMARY

Here is an example of a man who fought for what he knew was right. Who fought long and hard. And when he had won, there was no anger, no bitterness. He still did what was right for his people – *all* of his people.

We have seen that he started off as a young man in a good profession, always wanting to do the right thing; he had to leave that profession to follow a greater cause; he had to suffer for that cause, but he still did what he knew was right.

CLOSING

In this school we share a lot of values in common with this great man: we don't like bullies, we stand up for what is right and we, too, believe in reconciliation.

Notes:

AUTHORS

Mark Williams was Head of Science at St Georges School Edgbaston Birmingham. He now runs The Four Oaks tutor agency. He has written for Oxford University Press: The Association for Science Education, and was on the steering committee for the Perspectives on Science As level course. He has also written a light hearted book about The Hash House Harriers

Mike Venables. A former teacher of English and Drama, Mike is the Editor of Word Matters, the Journal of The Society of Teachers of Speech and Drama. He is President of Birmingham International Speakers and the owner of the training business, The Persuasive Speaking Company.

Luke Citrine Williams is the current Information Technology subject coordinator and a teacher of general Science at St George's English International School in Cologne, Germany. He graduated from Bradford University and received the Phil Davis prize. He undertook and completed his Post Graduate Certificate in Education at the University of Warwick.

Beryl Williams is retired teacher of Business Studies and Mathematics.

Bibliography / Websites

Summerhill School:
http://www.summerhillschool.co.uk/pages/index.html

Orders of magnitude:
http://en.wikipedia.org/wiki/Orders_of_magnitude_(energy)

Dyslexia:
http://www.thepowerofdyslexia.com/

Wikipedia:

http://en.wikipedia.org/wiki/Summerhill_School

http://en.wikipedia.org/wiki/John_Harrison

Predictions quotes:
http://www.etni.org.il/quotes/predictions.htm

(Thank you to Zoe Readhead for permission to quote from the Summerhill school website)

Printed by BoD™in Norderstedt, Germany